Smoothies & Juices

Smoothies & Juices

Techniques, equipment, ingredients and over
75 classic recipes shown in more than
200 truly stunning photographs

Joanna Farrow with photographs by Gus Filgate

aqua marine

Contents

A Liquid Revolution

Juices of one sort or another have been enjoyed for millennia, and shakes have been indulged in for decades, but the growing fascination with juicing and blending is something else again. Maybe this new liquid obsession is triggered by our growing interest in health and nutrition and the desire to improve our consumption of fresh fruit and vegetables, or because we've realized there's more to liquid refreshment than a carton of orange juice. Whatever the reasons, the fact remains that homemade smoothies, juices and blends are one of the most exciting things happening in today's kitchens.

The fast-moving world of kitchen technology has produced a vast range of affordable juicers, blenders and food processors that are all perfect for creating sumptuous, mouthwatering concoctions in your own home. No longer do we need to trek out to the health food store or juice bar for a freshly brewed blend, or feel restricted by the selection of hum drum juices on the supermarket shelves. If you fancy a glass of carrot, apple and orange juice, a shot of beetroot (beet) juice or a banana and mango smoothie, all you need to do is step into the kitchen, open the refrigerator and in a few minutes you can have the drink of your dreams at your fingertips.

The improved availability of seasonal and exotic ingredients has also opened up a whole range of possibilities to the juice or smoothie enthusiast. Once unusual or rarely available fruits, vegetables and flavourings can now be found on most supermarket shelves, often all year round. Juicing and blending can really make the most of these ingredients, bringing them together and turning them into fabulous fusions of flavour.

This book is committed to highly nutritious, energy-packed juice drinks, but also takes in some fun, out-of-the-ordinary treats. There is an enticing range of healthy, purifying juice blends as well as more inspired, flavoured juices that take in more interesting and unusual ingredients such as flower essences, exotic spices and aromatic syrups. Other deliciously indulgent recipes will satisfy a thirst for comfort and luxury. Try the dessert drinks, which tread the line between refreshing beverage and decadent after-dinner treat, or sample the irresistibly nostalgic frothy-topped milkshakes. Sip the best thick and creamy smoothies imaginable or impress guests with the outrageous alcoholic and non-alcoholic tipples that have been created with parties and entertaining in mind. All you need are some simple pieces of equipment, the freshest produce you can lay your hands on and a creative imagination.

Health kick

Modern juice extractors can squeeze the liquid and flavour from almost any fruit and vegetable in a matter of seconds. Provided you consume these juices almost as soon as you've made them, the incredible injection of vitamins and minerals that they offer is incomparable. The nutrients contained within fresh, raw fruits and vegetables also include valuable antioxidants that have the most incredible health-promoting potential.

Oxidation is now recognized as one of the main reasons for aging and is thought to cause a number of serious diseases and illnesses, so antioxidants really should be on everyone's daily list of must-have nutrients. Eating a diet with a high proportion of fresh fruits and vegetables can effectively decelerate the aging process and help prevent many of the life-threatening diseases that you're more likely to encounter as you get older – and juicing is one of the simplest ways to increase your consumption of fruit and vegetables.

So the moral of the story is clear: drink more fresh fruit and vegetable juices and you'll have a healthier, happier body. Just sip these wonder fluids and you can almost taste their goodness in the fresh, clean, cleansing flavours.

Quick-fix fun

In terms of short-term benefits, juicing and blending is a fast, fun and easy way to enjoy all your favourite flavours. Blending fruits with chilled yogurt, honey, milk, seeds and nuts can be amazingly quick, yet tastes great. The speed with which you can whip up these drinks makes them perfect for breakfast, or for quenching your thirst at any time of day. Just make sure you've got a good supply of raw ingredients chilling in the refrigerator so you can get blending whenever the mood takes you.

Don't be put off by the thought of all that peeling, chopping and preparation. Most ingredients need minimal preparation so the juice or smoothie can be ready to drink in a matter of minutes. From breakfast to bedtime, these delicious blends will offer the most fantastic liquid refreshment in an instant.

In the comfort zone

There are few things as wonderful as sitting back, relaxing and spoiling yourself with an edible treat just for the pure pleasure of it. A luxuriously creamy blended drink can be the perfect accessory to relaxation. Curl up on the sofa, or snuggle down in bed, with a freshly made juice or an indulgently rich smoothie or shake, and wallow in its divine taste and texture. Comfort drinks like these can be a total tonic and a fabulous way to escape from the manic pace of everyday life, transporting you into your own little oasis of calm.

Think of the most indulgent blend of smooth and succulent tropical fruits or the thickest, creamiest milkshake topped with scoops of vanilla ice cream – the sort you enjoyed as a child but somehow thought you should have grown out of. Imagine the tangiest, gloopiest fruit concoction, so thick that you need a spoon to drink it. Ingredients such as toffee and banana, rum and raisin, fragrant Turkish delight and melting milk chocolate make these drinks taste like they've been made in heaven – totally indulgent, definitely decadent and utterly irresistible.

The Basics

Juice extractors, blenders and food processors make light work of an otherwise laborious task. Making juices, smoothies and shakes has never been easier so all you need to worry about is preparing the ingredients (and cleaning up the mess).

Equipment

If you have the space it's well worth having both a blender and a juice extractor as they each produce quite different results. The juice extractor separates the juice from the pulp while the blender whizzes the whole fruit or vegetable to a purée, making a thicker drink. A sturdy food processor gives similar results to the blender but you often have to scrape the ingredients down the sides of the bowl and some models cannot be used for crushing ice.

Because there are now so many models of juicer and blender available it's worth looking around, seeking advice and experimenting (if you can) to find the one that's right for you. In most cases, the more you spend, the sturdier, more efficient and enduring your machine will be – an important consideration for the real blending fanatic. Whatever you choose, keep it on the work surface so it is always to hand when you feel like whizzing up a juice or smoothie.

Blenders liquidize whole ingredients, whereas juice extractors separate the juice from the pulp, producing a thinner drink.

Juice extractors

These miracle machines separate the fruit or vegetable juice from the pulp. The ingredients only need to be roughly chopped, then pushed into the machine. The pieces are mashed, then the juice and the pulp are separated by centrifugal force and the juice filtered into an integral container or glass. Most good electric juicers also have a cone-shaped attachment for juicing citrus fruits.

Extractors are great for getting the juice out of most fruits and even hard root vegetables. Because juice extractors remove the pulp from the juice, you'll get less volume than you would by blending the whole fruit or vegetable and the resulting juice is thin, often quite clear, and intensely flavoured. The percentage of juice extracted from the pulp can vary depending on the power of the machine; expensive commercial machines tend to extract a higher proportion of juice, leaving little waste.

Top-of-the-range models can be used to juice larger quantities before they need to be cleaned out. They tend to be bigger and bulkier but are built to last. For domestic use, there's value for money in many of the cheaper, more basic models. The main difference is that you can only juice a certain amount of fruits and vegetables before you have to stop and scrape out the pulp from the machine. You'll soon get a feel for how much can be juiced in one go – often the machine will start vibrating when it's had enough! More basic models may not have a citrus attachment, but don't be put off as it's just as easy to peel and chop the citrus fruit and push it through with the other ingredients.

The only negative aspect of these wonder machines is the cleaning up. It doesn't matter how much you spend on your machine or how deluxe the model, cleaning out a juicer is always a bit of a chore. However, the glorious juices that they produce are guaranteed to make it seem worthwhile. When buying a juicer you may like to consider that the more parts that can be popped in the dishwasher, the less time you'll need to spend at the kitchen sink.

Whatever you do though, remember that it's always easier to clean out a juicer that's just been used, rather than one that's been left sitting for a few hours with the pulp gradually welding itself to the machine.

Manual citrus juicers

For squeezing any citrus fruit, from limes to grapefruit, there are plenty of gadgets from which to choose. If you're just preparing one or two fruits, a stainless steel or glass hand squeezer is the quickest option. They're easy to use and quick to wash up. Use one with an effective pip (seed) collector and sufficiently large moat to catch the juice. Better still, use one that's set over a small bowl to catch the juices and minimize spillages.

There is also a wide range of slightly more sophisticated-looking and expensive chrome-plated free-standing extractors. These have a hinged arm that presses the fruit down on to the squeezer and presses the juice into a cup. They are great if you're pressing plenty of fruits but are a bit of an indulgence if it's only for squeezing the occasional lemon or lime. Most models have two squeezing cones, the smaller one for lemons and limes, the larger one for the larger fruits such as oranges and grapefruit.

Free-standing citrus presses are great for juicing large quantities and offer the added bonus of looking incredibly sophisticated.

Blenders & liquidizers

Domestic blenders have been around for much longer than juice extractors and there's a huge selection on the market, varying greatly in motor power, speed settings and jug capacity. Some of the sturdier models have an ice-crushing setting, which is worth considering if you intend to make plenty of long summer drinks and cocktails. Unlike juice extractors, blenders and liquidizers purée the ingredients so that more juice is made.

Before blending, all fruits and vegetables must be thoroughly washed or peeled. Cut away any damaged parts and cores, seeds and stones (pits), then chop the flesh into chunks. Because the blended juice is thick it often needs the addition of citrus juice or water to dilute it. Fruits such as bananas, mangoes and avocados are far better whizzed up in a blender than a juicer.

Hand-held electric wands

Although more widely used for blending soups, sauces and purées, these slender, hand-held electric blenders and whisks are great for mixing and frothing up creamy drinks and milkshakes. They are not suitable for blending hard ingredients such as apples or root vegetables.

Food processors

These are more of an all-round kitchen gadget, but they're also good for blending drinks. Bigger models are great for large quantities. Food processors tend to create more washing up than blenders and liquidizers and they take up extra space on the work surface but, if you have one already, you may want to stick with it. Don't use food processors for crushing ice unless the model states that you can. Some food processors have a citrus juicer attachment, which can be useful for pressing large quantities of fruit.

Food processors are great for blending large quantities, while hand-held electric blenders are ideal for whizzing up single portions.

Other useful equipment

Vegetable peeler — Search out a good quality peeler that will only take off a thin layer of peel without damaging the flesh.

Grater — You will need a sharp box or hand-held grater that'll effortlessly remove citrus fruit rind, and grate ginger.

Chopping board — Choose a sturdy board that won't slide around during use. Keep a separate board for chopping fruit so it doesn't pick up the flavours of other ingredients.

Knives — Make sure you have a couple of sharp knives, including one that's strong enough to chop larger fruits such as melons and pineapple.

Jugs/pitchers — A good selection of measuring and serving jugs are useful for making and serving juices and smoothies. They are also good for storing drinks; just cover with clear film (plastic wrap) and place in the refrigerator.

Scrubbing brush — Keep a small lightweight brush for scrubbing fruit and vegetables that you don't want to peel.

Kitchen scales — These are useful for making specific juice and smoothie recipes where a measured quantity is needed.

Different fruits and vegetables require different preparation: some should be peeled, others washed thoroughly and some chopped.

Making the most of it

To maximize the flavour and goodness of your drinks, take care to follow these preparation guidelines.

Use only very fresh produce — Fruit and vegetables that have been hanging around on the supermarket shelves or in your refrigerator for days, will have lost much of their nutritional value, as well as flavour. Avoid damaged or reduced-price produce. A greengrocer is often a good source of fresh produce.

Where possible, buy organic produce — However, do be selective as organic fruits and vegetables can also be kept on supermarket shelves for too long.

Refrigerate — Most fruit and vegetables are best kept in the refrigerator and should be used as soon as possible after purchase.

Make the most of home-grown produce — If you have a glut of apples, pears, plums, soft fruits or tomatoes, they can be juiced singly and frozen. Pack the juice in thoroughly clean cartons or well sealed, heavy-duty plastic bags.

Scrub or wash it well — If you're not peeling produce, it should be washed very well. Non-organic ingredients should be washed in soapy water then rinsed, as chemicals and pesticides can cling firmly to the skins of fruits and vegetables.

Don't overchop — Only chop fruit and vegetables as finely as you need to feed them into the machine. The more you chop the more you risk destroying the nutrients they contain. Only chop ingredients as and when you need to juice.

Start with small ingredients — If you're juicing small quantities of an ingredient or those with an intense flavour such as herbs and ginger, push them through at the beginning or halfway through the process.

Cool or chilled — Juices should be drunk as soon as they're ready, so juice ingredients at the temperature you like to drink them. If you like your juice really cold, chill the fruits and vegetables until ready to use, but bear in mind that underripe fruit won't ripen very well in the refrigerator. (Remember that banana skins will turn black if the fruits are stored in the refrigerator.)

Choosing & using fruits

Apples — A good source of vitamin C and calcium, and good all-round juicers. They are delicious on their own or mixed with other fruits and most vegetables. If the apples are non-organic, wash them well, gently scrubbing the skins to remove as many of the external chemicals as possible. Roughly chop the flesh.

Apricots — A good source of iron, fibre and vitamins A and C. Wash, halve and stone (pit). Choose plump fruits with a fairly firm, smooth skin.

Bananas — A good energy food that is high in fibre and minerals. Use when the skin is yellow or brown specked. They are great for blending but should not be used for juicing.

Soft summer fruits are great blended with yogurt to make smoothies, while fresh salad vegetables are better juiced on their own, or with other vegetables or mild, crisp fruits.

Blackberries — A good source of vitamin C, calcium and minerals. Juice raw or cook very briefly in sugar syrup to soften.

Cherries — A good cleansing fruit that is rich in vitamin C and calcium. Pit before juicing. If you use a lot of cherries, a cherry pitter will take much of the effort out of their preparation.

Citrus fruits — Rich in vitamin C as well as calcium and minerals. One or two fruits are easier squeezed using a hand juicer. Use an electric juicer for larger quantities; cut away the skins and put the flesh through the juice extractor. Some recipes use the whole chopped fruit, including the skins, which will give the juice a very strong, distinctive flavour.

Cranberries — High in vitamin C and a good internal cleanser, cranberries have a sharp and slightly astringent flavour. Juice whole.

Grapes — Rich in antioxidants but not vitamins. Quality grapes, full of natural sugar, make deliciously sweet juices, but some can be sharp or sour. Juice whole, discarding the stalks.

Mangoes — High in fibre and vitamins A and C, mangoes are better blended than juiced. Ripe fruit will be strongly scented and give when gently pressed. Halve, stone (pit) and scoop out the flesh.

Melons — A high water content makes this a good rehydrating fruit. It contains small amounts of vitamins and blends well with other fruits. Scoop out the seeds and remove the skin before juicing or blending.

Passion fruit — Only use fruits that are brown and slightly dimpled. A very wrinkled skin is usually a sign of age. Halve the fruits and press the pulp through a sieve before adding to drinks if you don't like the seeds.

Peaches — A good source of vitamin C, peaches are only worth juicing or blending when really ripe as this brings out their sweet flavour. Remove stones (pits) and skin if blending. To peel peaches, blanch the briefly in boiling water, then lift off the skin with the point of a sharp knife. It should peel away easily.

Pears — Like apples, pears juice really well and blend with other fruit and vegetables, providing plenty of natural sweetness and a delicate, aromatic flavour. Prepare in the same way as apples.

Pineapple — A ripe fruit should smell sweet and aromatic. Cut away the thick skin and discard the core before blending or juicing. Pineapples are high in natural sugar and vitamin C.

Plums — These are often underripe when bought so leave at room temperature to ripen (this may take several days). Wash well and stone (pit) but don't peel. Prepare greengages and damsons in the same way.

Raspberries — A good source of vitamins, calcium and minerals, raspberries make a delicious juice, blended singly or with other soft fruits and peaches. Wash just before use only if necessary.

Strawberries — Rich in vitamin C and natural sugar. Strawberries make a fabulous juice, blended with other fruits or served on its own. Don't bother hulling the fruits before juicing, but halve any large ones.

Juicy watermelon can be blended or juiced; aromatic spices can be used to make syrups to flavour juices or smoothies.

Many vegetables contain high levels of natural sugars and can be juiced to produce the sweetest, most delicious juices. Freshly made vegetable juices often have a really clean taste and are good blended with fruit juices.

Choosing & using veg

Avocados — Although high in vitamins, minerals and protein, avocados are also packed with calories so don't overdo them if you're trying to lose weight. Only use if the skin gives a little when gently pressed. Underripe avocados can be stored in the fruit bowl with a banana until softened but keep an eye on them as they'll soon be past their best once ripened. Halve and scoop out the flesh discarding the stone (pit). Avocados are far better blended than juiced.

Beetroot/beets — Although beetroot leaves can be cooked like cabbage, it's the roots that are the most interesting to use. Rich in nutrients, beetroot is a great cleanser and juices really well. Scrub and roughly chop before use.

Broccoli — An excellent antioxidant, broccoli is high in vitamins and other nutrients. Wash thoroughly in cold water before use and discard the tough stalks before juicing.

Carrots — Young carrots have the best flavour and texture for juicing. Peel before juicing to make a naturally sweet drink that's particularly high in vitamin A and blends well with other vegetables and fruits.

Celery — Separate the sticks and wash well before using to remove any specks of grit. Blend the leaves too, or use leafy stalks as drink stirrers.

Cucumber — These have a very high water content (about 90%) and a lower nutritional value than most other vegetables. Pushed through the juicer though, cucumber has a surprisingly strong taste and can be peeled first for a lighter, more refreshing flavour.

Fennel — The fennel bulb makes a refreshing juice with a mild aniseed flavour. Use the whole bulb and any feathery fronds attached to it.

Lettuce — The refreshing leaves wilt and quickly lose their nutritional content during storage so are best used as fresh as possible. Lettuce makes an intensely flavoured juice that's good blended with milder tasting fruits and vegetables.

Parsnips — Scrubbed or peeled and pushed through the juicer, young parsnips have a deliciously milky, sweet flavour that blends well with most other fruits and vegetables. A good source of vitamins and fibre.

Peppers/bell peppers — Rich in vitamins C and A, peppers make a great juice on their own or blended with other fruits and vegetables. Cut away the stalks but don't worry about seeding them.

Radishes — Crisp and peppery, radishes make a vibrant addition to juice blends.

Tomatoes — Rich in vitamins, tomatoes mix well with other fruits and vegetables. Skin first for blending. Chop roughly for juicing.

Watercress — Rich in vitamins C and A as well as minerals, watercress is a good natural cleanser and aid to digestion. Use as fresh as possible as it spoils quickly, even when stored in the refrigerator.

Juice boosts

Invigorating blends of fruits and vegetables are naturally packed with goodness, but there are plenty of additional supplements, available from chemists and health food stores, that you might want to add to your juice, whether it's to boost general vitality or aid recovery, or simply for enjoyment. Read the label before use to check suitability and recommended doses. In most cases, just a few drops are added so the flavour or consistency of the drink won't be affected. These are some of the most readily available.

Brewer's yeast — A rich source of B vitamins and minerals and an excellent supplement for increased vitality.

Echinacea — This herb and root blend is taken both for the prevention and cure of colds and flu. Echinacea is good antiseptic tonic for circulation and respiration.

Ginkgo biloba — A homeopathic supplement that comes from one of the most ancient known Asian trees. Ginkgo biloba aids digestion, helps combat allergies and breathing problems and improves blood circulation. Because of this it's also supposed to improve memory and brain function.

Ginseng — Another Asian cure-all, this herb has many health-giving properties, helping mainly in strengthening the immune system. It also aids recovery from illness and can help with stress. American ginseng has similar properties.

Kelp — Available in powder form, this seaweed is an excellent source of iron.

Spirulina — This microscopic seaweed, high in protein and other vital nutrients, is estimated to have existed for over three billion years. It's packed with minerals and is said to contain 25 times the amount of betacarotene in carrots.

Wheatgrass — Grown from the wheat berry, wheatgrass is a concentrated source of chlorophyll and valuable nutrients with many health-giving properties.

Fresh herbs can be used to flavour drinks; wheatgrass can be juiced on its own to make a potent detoxifier.

Keeping it creamy

Coconut milk— The ultimate dairy-free decadence. Use canned coconut milk or freshly juiced coconut to add a really rich element to smoothies and shakes.

Ice cream— Add to smoothies or shakes before serving or mix into drinks to make a thick, frosty blend. Always choose a really good quality ice cream as cheaper brands tend to taste thin and synthetic, particularly when blended.

Milk— Use full cream (whole) milk unless you want a lighter, lower fat drink.

Soya milk— If you want to make a dairy-free drink that's still wonderfully rich and creamy, soya milk works particularly well. Sweetened and unsweetened varieties are widely available in most supermarkets.

Yogurt— Natural (plain), Greek (US strained plain) and live bio yogurt are all great in smoothies and shakes. Their slightly acidic flavour produces a creamy drink with a fresh and tangy taste.

Serve in style

Making quick and easy juices and smoothies isn't about highly decorated glasses and garnishes. But you might just want to add a decorative twist to a summer cooler or cocktail, particularly for larger parties.

Herb flower ice cubes — Lay freshly picked herb flowers, such as borage, thyme, mint, rosemary, sage or lavender into sections of an ice-cube tray. Fill with water and freeze until required.

Whole fruit ice cubes — Make as for herb flower ice cubes using small whole fresh fruits, such as cranberries, raspberries and redcurrants instead.

Iced fruit cubes — Juice or fruit purée can be frozen in cubes. This is useful if you have juice left over or you want to chill drinks without diluting the flavour.

Crushed ice — Make sure your food processor or blender is designed to crush ice, otherwise you may damage the blade and the motor. If it isn't suitable, use the traditional method: put ice cubes in a double-thickness plastic bag and beat furiously with a rolling pin. Return the ice to the freezer until needed.

Sugared or salted glasses — Sugar- or salt-encrusted glass rims look very pretty. Put a little caster (superfine) sugar or salt in a saucer. Using your finger, run a little lemon juice around the rim of the glass then invert the rim into the sugar.

Perfect blends

Some of the simplest combinations of fruit and vegetables make deliciously healthy and appetizing drinks. Use these simple ideas to inspire your own combinations. Each blend makes one serving.

Fruit/vegetable	Quantities	Preparation	Method
Apple and pear	1 large apple 1 large pear	Roughly chop	Juice together
Banana and lime	1 large banana 2 limes	Peel and chop banana. Squeeze limes	Blend together and dilute with mineral water
Cranberry and melon	100g/3¾oz/scant 1 cup cranberries large wedge melon	Skin melon and cut into chunks	Juice cranberries, then melon
Beetroot and carrot	1 beetroot (beet) 2 carrots	Peel carrots, roughly chop both	Juice together
Carrot and ginger	4 carrots 1cm/½in piece fresh root ginger	Peel carrots and roughly chop. Roughly chop ginger	Juice ginger, then carrots
Fennel and apple	1 small fennel bulb 2 small apples	Roughly chop	Juice together
Hot tomato	250g/9oz tomatoes 1 lemon ground black pepper	Skin and chop tomatoes. Squeeze lemon	Blend tomatoes, add lemon juice and pepper
Iceberg and grape	½ iceberg lettuce 200g/7oz/1¾ cups green grapes	Roughly chop lettuce	Juice together
Mango and orange	1 small mango 1 large orange	Halve and stone (pit) mango, scoop out flesh. Juice orange	Blend mango, then blend in orange
Orchard fruits	4 large red plums 4 greengages 1 small apple	Stone (pit) plums and greengages. Roughly chop apple	Juice together
Pear and cucumber	1 large pear ½ small cucumber	Roughly chop pear. Peel and chop cucumber	Juice together
Strawberry and orange	250g/9oz/2¼ cups strawberries 1 large orange	Chop any large strawberries. Squeeze orange	Juice strawberries, add orange
Triple citrus	1 grapefruit 1 large orange 1 lime	Halve	Squeeze and mix together
Watercress and apple	2 small apples small handful of watercress	Roughly chop apples	Juice watercress then apples

Fresh & Raw

These are the healthiest of all the blends, using only the freshest, rawest, juiciest ingredients. Each fruit and vegetable concoction combines juices that are cleansing, nourishing, energizing, refreshing – and ultimately delicious. To really reap the benefits, drink them the moment they've been made.

Pink & perky

This deliciously refreshing rose-tinged blend of grapefruit and pear juice will keep you bright-eyed and bushy-tailed. It's perfect for breakfast or as a pick-me-up when energy levels are flagging. If the grapefruit are particularly tart, serve with a little bowl of brown sugar, or even brown sugar stirrers.

Makes 2 tall glasses

2 pink grapefruit, halved

2 ripe pears

ice cubes

Take a thin slice from one grapefruit half and halve it. Squeeze all the juice from the halves. Cut a few thin slices of pear. Roughly chop the rest and push through the juicer.

Mix the fruit juices together and serve in tall glasses over ice. Decorate with the grapefruit and pear slices.

Sweet, sharp shock

The taste-tingling combination of red grape and tart apple is quite delicious. Grapes are full of natural sugars and, mixed with apple juice, they'll create a juice that's full of pep and zing. Grapes are also renowned for their cleansing properties, making this an ideal addition to any detox regime. For a longer, more refreshing drink, top up with sparkling mineral water.

Makes 1 large glass

150g/5oz/1¼ cups red grapes

1 red-skinned eating apple

1 small cooking apple

crushed ice

Slice some grapes and a sliver or two of apple for the decoration. Roughly chop the remaining apples. Push through a juicer with the grapes.

Pour over crushed ice, decorate with the sliced fruit and serve immediately.

The simplest flavour combinations are often the most divine. Sugary grapes and mouth-puckeringly tart apples are one of those perfect pairings that simply can't be beaten.

Minty melon soother

The wonderfully juicy flesh of ripe melon seems somehow more fragrant and sweet when juiced. A dash of lime cuts through the sweetness and zips up the flavour while refreshing, peppery mint makes a classic companion to both. This mellow soother is at once calming and stimulating.

Makes 3–4 glasses

1 Galia or cantaloupe melon

several large mint sprigs

juice of 2 large limes

ice cubes

extra mint sprigs and lime slices, to decorate

Halve and seed the melon and cut into wedges. Cut one wedge into long, thin slices and reserve for decoration.

Cut the skin from the remaining wedges and push half the melon through a juicer. Strip the mint leaves from the sprigs, push them through, then juice the remaining melon.

Stir in the lime juice and pour over ice cubes in glasses. Decorate with mint sprigs and lime slices. Add a slice of melon to each glass and serve immediately.

Mouthwateringly smooth, glistening melon wedges are guaranteed to produce the sweetest most refreshing juice imaginable.

Bright eyes

Thin-skinned citrus fruits like clementines can be put through the juicer without peeling, adding a zesty kick to the final mix – and saving time when you're in a hurry. This vibrant, intensely flavoured carrot and clementine combination is packed with vitamin A, which is essential for healthy vision, and vitamin C to boost the whole system.

Makes 2 glasses

6 clementines

200g/7oz carrots

ice cubes

Quarter the clementines, discarding any pips (seeds). Scrub the carrots and chop them into large chunks of more or less the same size.

Push the clementines through a juicer, then repeat the procedure with the carrots. Pour the juice over ice cubes in tall glasses and decorate with a wedge or slice of clementine, if you like.

Extra zing — Take the tingle factor up a notch by spicing up the mix. Peel and slice a little fresh root ginger and juice with the fruit and carrots.

Smooth yet sassy, with all the colour of a golden sunrise, this mouthwatering juice makes waking up worthwhile – even on the most sluggish morning.

Ruby roots

Beetroot has the highest sugar content of any vegetable and, not surprisingly, makes one of the most fabulously delicious juices with a vibrant red colour and rich but refreshing taste. Despite its firmness, it can be juiced raw and its intense flavour goes wonderfully with tangy citrus fruits and fresh root ginger. Enjoy this juice as a natural cleanser.

Makes 1 large glass

200g/7oz raw beetroot (beets)

1cm/½in piece fresh root ginger, peeled

1 large orange

ice cubes

Trim the beetroot and cut them in quarters. Push half the beetroot through the juicer, followed by the ginger and remaining beetroot.

Squeeze the juice from the orange, using a citrus juicer or by hand and mix with the beetroot juice in a jug (pitcher).

Pour over ice cubes in a glass or clear glass cup, so the full beauty of the rich colour can be appreciated. Serve immediately. Do not let the ice cubes melt into the drink or they will dilute it.

Blood-red beetroot produces a vibrant, shockingly intense, jewel-coloured juice that is packed with vitamins and minerals, making it the perfect tonic and ultimate health juice.

Celery sensation

Savoury, almost salty celery and sweet, green grapes make an astoundingly effective twosome when combined in a blended juice. A small handful of peppery watercress adds an extra punch, but be careful not to add too much, as its flavour intensifies considerably when the leaves are juiced.

Makes 1 large glass

2 celery sticks

a handful of watercress

200g/7oz/1¾ cups green grapes

1 leafy celery stick, to serve

crushed ice

Push the celery through a juicer, then follow with the watercress and grapes.

Put a leafy celery stick in a large glass and half fill with crushed ice. Pour the juice over the ice and serve.

Swizzle— The juice is liable to separate when left to stand so, just before drinking, stir it with the celery stick, which makes an excellent, edible swizzle stick.

Sugar snap

Sweet and juicy sugar snap peas are one of the most delicious vegetables to serve raw and taste just as good when put through the juicer. The sweetness of the peas and the melon intensifies when they are juiced and the fresh root ginger adds a certain edge in this mellow, cooling juice.

Makes 1 large glass

¼ honeydew or Galia melon

1cm/½in piece fresh root ginger, peeled

200g/7oz sugar snap peas

Scoop out the seeds from the melon and cut into wedges. Cut away and discard the skin, then chop the flesh into chunks. Chop the ginger.

Push the sugar snap peas (pods and all), through a juicer, then follow with the ginger and melon. Serve chilled.

Parsnip pep

Parsnips yield a relatively small amount of juice, but what the juicer produces is amazingly thick, sweet and creamy, perfect for adding body to any raw fruit and vegetable blends. Refreshing fennel, apple and pear are the perfect foils for the intense sweetness of the parsnip juice and will go on to produce the most tantalizing power-pack of a juice.

Makes 2 glasses

200g/7oz parsnips

125g/4¼oz fennel

1 apple

1 pear

a small handful of fresh flat leaf parsley

crushed ice

Cut the parsnips and fennel into large chunks. Quarter the apple and pear, then cut the pieces in half.

Push half the prepared fruit and vegetables through a juicer, then follow with the parsley and the remaining fruit and vegetables.

Fill short glasses with ice and pour the juice over. Serve immediately for maximum nutritional impact.

Parsnips are at their sweetest a few weeks after the first frost so try a shot of this wonderful juice when you're in need of a little winter boost.

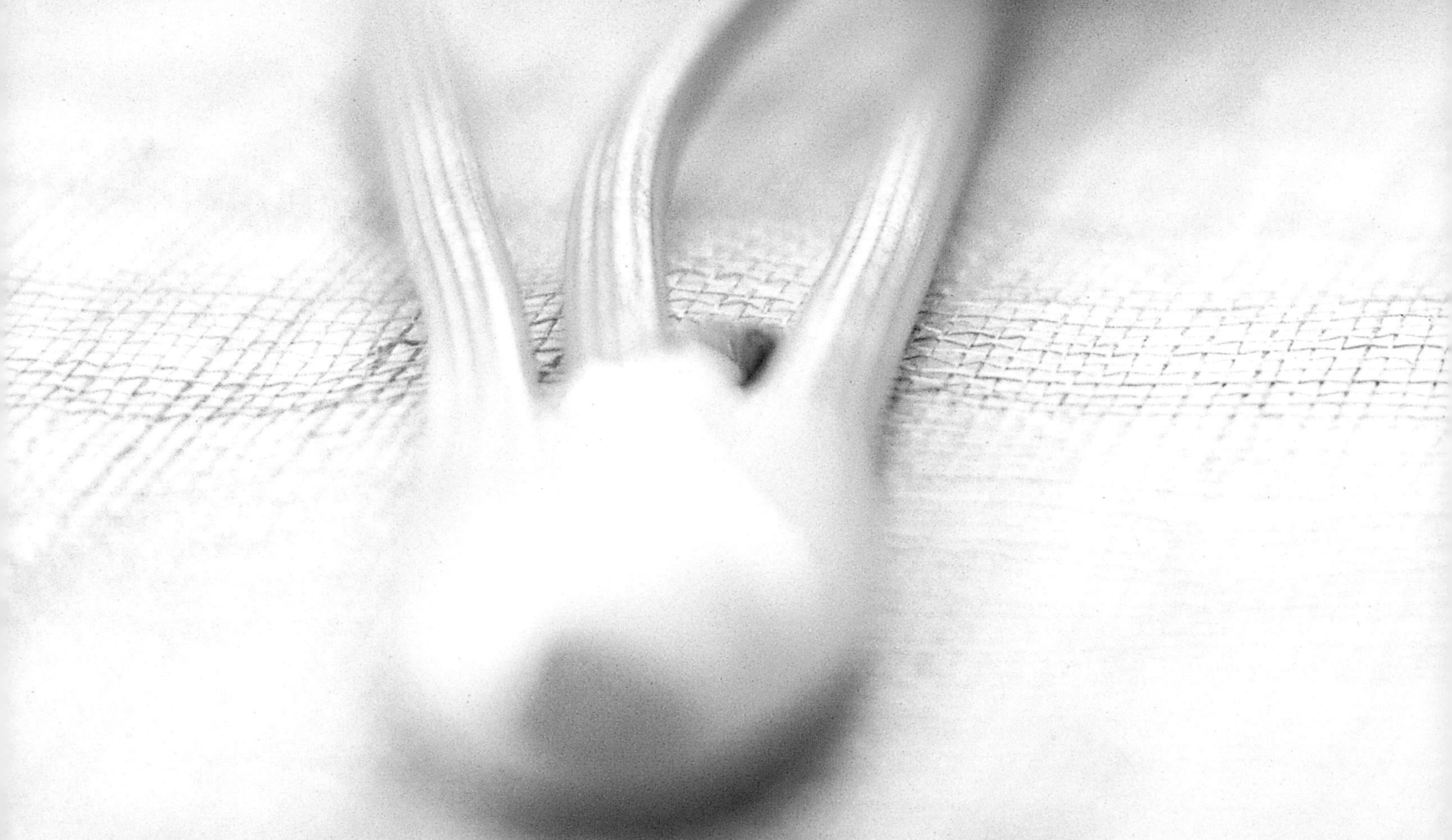

Broccoli booster

Broccoli has been hailed as a cure-all "superfood" and a vital ingredient in a healthy diet, but its strong taste does need a bit of toning down when juiced. Sweet and tangy apples soften its flavour, making a drink that's thoroughly enjoyable.

Makes 1 large glass

125g/4¼oz broccoli florets

2 eating apples

15ml/1 tbsp lemon juice

ice cubes

If large, cut the broccoli florets into smaller pieces. Chop the apples.

Push both through a juicer and stir in the lemon juice. Serve in a tall glass with plenty of ice.

Flavour-saver— Don't use the tough broccoli stalks as they provide little juice and don't have as good a flavour as the delicate florets.

Broccoli is packed with antiviral and antibacterial nutrients and contains almost as much calcium as milk. It is also thought to prevent some cancers, so this is definitely worth drinking.

Red hot chilli pepper

Sweet red peppers make a colourful, light juice that's best mixed with other ingredients for a full flavour impact. Courgettes add a subtle, almost unnoticeable body to the drink, while chilli and radishes add a wonderful edge of peppery heat. Freshly squeezed orange gives a delicious zest to this eminently drinkable beverage.

Makes 2–3 glasses

150g/5oz courgettes (zucchini)

2 red (bell) peppers

1 fresh red chilli, seeded

75g/3oz radishes

1 orange

ice cubes

Cut the courgettes into chunks and push them through a juicer. Halve the red peppers, remove the cores and seeds, and quarter the pieces. Juice them with the chilli, then halve the radishes and push them through.

Squeeze the orange and stir the juice into the vegetable juice. Fill two or three glasses with ice, pour over the juice and serve immediately.

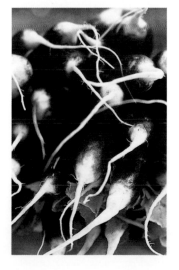

Basil blush

Some herbs just don't juice well, losing their aromatic flavour and turning muddy and dull. Basil, on the other hand, is an excellent juicer, keeping its distinctive fresh fragrance. It makes the perfect partner for mild, refreshing cucumber and the ripest, juiciest tomatoes you can find.

Makes 1 tall glass

½ cucumber, peeled

a handful of fresh basil

350g/12oz tomatoes

ice cubes

basil sprigs, to decorate

Quarter the cucumber lengthways. There's no need to remove the seeds. Push it through a juicer with the basil, then do the same with the tomatoes.

Pour the tomato, basil and cucumber juice over ice in one tall or two short glasses and echo the herb flavour by serving with a few basil sprigs.

Fresh and sweet— You don't have to peel the cucumber, but it gives the juice a fresher, lighter colour. If you're feeling indulgent, use cherry tomatoes for their extra sweet flavour.

Sun-ripened tomatoes, freshly picked basil and cool, refreshing cucumber make a smooth, thick juice that is rich with the intense flavours of summer.

Gazpacho juice

Inspired by the classic Spanish soup, this fabulous juice looks and tastes delicious. Fresh salad vegetables can be thrown into a blender and whizzed up in moments to create a refreshing, invigorating drink, or even a cooling *al fresco* appetizer on a hot summer's day.

Makes 4–5 glasses

800g/1¾lb tomatoes, skinned

½ cucumber, roughly sliced

1 red (bell) pepper, seeded and cut into chunks

1 celery stick, chopped

1 spring onion (scallion), roughly chopped

½ fresh red chilli

a small handful of fresh coriander (cilantro), plus extra to decorate

juice of 1 lime

salt

Put the tomatoes, cucumber, red pepper, celery and spring onion in a food processor or blender. Remove and discard the seeds from the chilli and add to the other vegetables, along with the coriander. Blend well until completely liquid, scraping the mixture down from the sides of the bowl if necessary.

Add the lime juice and a little salt to the juice and blend briefly to combine. Pour into glasses and add ice cubes and a few coriander leaves to serve.

Fluid and flavour— Stir in a little extra tomato juice or mineral water if the juice is still thick after blending. A splash of red wine vinegar will intensify the flavour.

Juices made from salad vegetables are the ultimate thirst quenchers on a hot day, offering wonderfully fresh flavours and valuable nutrients.

Fruity & Refreshing

Take juicing one step further by adding exciting, enticing, aromatic flavours – lavender with orange, star anise with watermelon, juniper with rhubarb, or stem ginger with kiwi. Why stop at the basic when there's such a wonderful array of fabulous fusions and flavours to explore?

Strawberry & apple slush

Sweet, juicy strawberries make wonderfully fragrant juices, with a consistency that's not too thick, not too thin. The addition of apple juice and just a hint of vanilla creates a tantalizing treat that's perfect for sipping on a lazy summer's afternoon.

Makes 2 tall glasses

300g/11oz/2½ cups ripe strawberries

2 small, crisp eating apples

10ml/2 tsp vanilla syrup

crushed ice

Pick out a couple of the prettiest strawberries and reserve for the decoration. Hull the remaining strawberries and roughly chop the apples into large chunks.

Push the fruits through a juicer and stir in the vanilla syrup.

Half-fill two tall glasses with ice. Add straws or stirrers and pour over the juice. Decorate with the reserved strawberries (slicing them if you like) and serve immediately.

Searching for syrup—Sweet vanilla syrup can be bought in jars from supermarkets and delicatessens. As an alternative, add a few drops of vanilla essence (extract) and a sprinkling of sugar if necessary.

Berried treasure

Cranberries and raspberries are fast becoming a juice classic, despite the fact that they're each at their best during different seasons. This needn't hinder you though, just use one in frozen form – the fruit will thaw quickly and save you adding ice. This recipe uses raspberry conserve to add the necessary sweetness, in place of the more usual sugar or honey.

Makes 2 tall glasses

250g/9oz/1¼ cups raspberries

45ml/3 tbsp raspberry conserve

250g/9oz/1½ cups cranberries

soda water (club soda) or sparkling mineral water

Push all the raspberries through a juicer, then do the same with the raspberry conserve and cranberries.

Pour the juice into tall glasses and top up with soda water or sparkling mineral water and serve immediately.

Berry spikes — For presentation, try threading a few of the berries on to wooden cocktail sticks (toothpicks) and rest across the rim of the glasses. (To balance the sticks successfully, you'll need to use relatively narrow glasses or the sticks may fall in.)

Cherry berry trio

Strawberries and grapes have long been reputed to cleanse and purify the system, while cherries and strawberries are rich in vitamin C. This trio of plump, ripe fruits is packed with natural fruit sugars and needs absolutely no sweetening. To really spoil yourself (and undo all that cleansing power), try adding a splash of your favourite orange liqueur.

Makes 2 large glasses

200g/7oz/1¾ cups strawberries

250g/9oz/2¼ cups red grapes

150g/5oz/1¼ cups red cherries, pitted

ice cubes

Halve two or three strawberries and grapes and set aside with a few perfect cherries for decoration. Cut up any large strawberries, then push through a juicer with the remaining grapes and cherries.

Pour into glasses, top with the halved fruits, cherries and ice cubes, and serve immediately. For a fun decoration, skewer a halved strawberry or grape on a cocktail stick (toothpick) and hang a cherry by its stem.

Each year, the cherry season passes all too swiftly, so enjoy them in their full glory in this refreshing blend of sweet, fruity, fragrant red juices.

Passion fruit & orange crush

The scent and taste of this juice achieves that hard-to-reach balance of aromas and flavours. Sweet, zesty orange juice sits in perfect harmony with aromatic cardamom and intensely fragrant passion fruit to make the most heavenly juice imaginable. And as well as the fabulous flavour and glorious colour, you get a generous shot of health-giving vitamin C.

Makes 2 glasses

15ml/1 tbsp cardamom pods

15ml/1 tbsp caster (superfine) sugar

4 large oranges

2 passion fruit

ice cubes

halved orange slices, to decorate

Crush the cardamom pods in a mortar with a pestle or place them in a small, metal bowl and pound with the end of a rolling pin until the seeds are exposed.

Tip the cardamom pods, with any seeds that have escaped, into a small pan. Add the sugar and stir in 90ml/6 tbsp water. Cover the pan and simmer gently for about 5 minutes.

Squeeze the oranges in a citrus juicer or by hand and tip the juice into a small jug (pitcher). Halve the passion fruit and scoop the pulp into the jug. Strain the cardamom syrup through a fine sieve into the fruit juice and whisk the mixture to distribute the passion fruit and make a light froth.

Half-fill tall glasses with ice cubes and pour over the juice. Slip the orange slices into the glasses to serve as edible decoration.

Seed sense — The seeds in passion fruit look pretty suspended in the juice and are perfectly edible, but they don't offer any nutrition and can get suck between your teeth. If you don't want them in the drink, press the pulp through a small sieve and just use the juice.

Sweet yet sharp, delicate yet robust, mouth-puckering yet refreshing – each sip of this unbelievably delicious juice plays with every sense.

Watermelon & star anise fizz

The delicate taste of watermelon becomes surprisingly intense when juiced, so additional flavours need to be equally pronounced. A light syrup infused with scented star anise is the perfect choice. For maximum impact, make sure the star anise is really fresh as its liquorice-like flavour and aroma tend to fade with age.

Makes 2 tall glasses

15g/½oz star anise

15ml/1 tbsp caster (superfine) sugar

500g/1¼lb wedge watermelon

sparkling mineral water

Roughly crush the star anise in a mortar using a pestle, or place it in a small metal bowl and pound with the end of a rolling pin.

Tip the crushed spice into a small pan and add the sugar and 90ml/6 tbsp water. Bring to the boil, stirring, then let it bubble for 2 minutes. Remove from the heat and leave to steep for 10 minutes.

Cut off and discard the rind from the melon and cut the flesh into chunks, removing the hard black seeds.

Push the melon through a juicer. Strain the anise syrup through a fine sieve and pour it into the melon juice. Stir well to mix.

Fill the glasses two-thirds full with the juice. Top up with sparkling water and serve immediately.

Sweet, scented, frothy pink bubbles make this heavenly juice the perfect choice for a non-alcoholic cocktail. Or enjoy as a cooling thirst-quencher on a long, hot summer afternoon.

Kiwi & stem ginger spritzer

The delicate, refreshingly tangy flavour of kiwi fruit becomes sweeter and more intense when the flesh is juiced. Choose plump, unwrinkled fruits that give a little when gently pressed as underripe fruits will produce a juice with a slightly bitter taste. A single kiwi fruit contains more than a single day's vitamin C requirement so this juice will really boost the system.

Makes 1 tall glass

1 piece preserved stem ginger, plus 15ml/1 tbsp syrup from the ginger jar

2 kiwi fruit

sparkling mineral water

Chop the ginger and roughly chop the kiwi fruit. (For a better colour you can peel the fruit first, but this isn't essential.)

Push the ginger, and then the kiwi fruit, through a juicer and pour it into a jug (pitcher). Stir in the ginger syrup.

Pour the juice into a tall glass, then top up with sparkling mineral water and serve immediately.

Apple infusion

East meets West with this fabulous fusion of fresh apple and fragrant spices. Apple and ginger juice is combined with fragrant lemon grass to make a deliciously refreshing cooler. It's well worth making a double quantity and keeping a supply in the refrigerator.

Makes 2–3 glasses

1 lemon grass stalk

15g/½oz fresh root ginger, peeled

4 red-skinned eating apples

ice cubes

red apple slices, to decorate

sparkling water or real lemonade

Bruise the lemon grass stalk by pounding it with the tip of a rolling pin. Make several lengthways cuts through the stalk to open it up, keeping it intact at the thick end. Put the bruised stem into a small glass jug (pitcher).

Roughly chop the ginger and cut the apples into chunks. Push the ginger and then the apples through a juicer.

Pour the juice into the jug and place in the refrigerator for at least 1 hour to let the flavours infuse.

Half-fill glasses with ice cubes and red apple slices and pour in the juice to just cover the ice. Top up with sparkling water or lemonade and serve immediately.

The subtle flavour of lemon grass pervades this sparkling apple and ginger cooler to create the ultimate thirst-quencher with a hint of the East.

Pink "gin"

Juniper berries are a vital ingredient in the making of gin and, not surprisingly, they exude distinct gin-like aromas in this fabulous drink. For a good colour, this is best made using early "forced" rhubarb, which gives the juice a characteristic pink blush. Top up the "gin" with sparkling water, or use real lemonade for a really tangy taste.

Makes 4 glasses

600g/1lb 6oz rhubarb

finely grated rind and juice of 2 limes

75g/3oz/6 tbsp caster (superfine) sugar

15ml/1 tbsp juniper berries, lightly crushed

ice cubes

lime slices, quartered

sparkling mineral water, soda water (club soda) or real lemonade

Using a sharp knife, chop the rhubarb into 2cm/¾in lengths and place in a pan with the lime rind and juice, sugar, crushed juniper berries and 90ml/6 tbsp water. Cover with a tightly fitting lid and cook for 6–8 minutes until the rhubarb is just tender. (Test by prodding with the tip of a knife.)

Transfer the rhubarb to a food processor or blender and process to form a smooth purée. Press the mixture through a coarse sieve into a bowl and set the strained juice aside until completely cooled.

Half-fill medium glasses with the juice. Add ice cubes and lime slices and top up with sparkling mineral water, soda water or lemonade. Serve immediately.

Intensifying the taste — If the rhubarb syrup is stored for a couple of days in the refrigerator after straining, the juniper flavour will become more pronounced. The overall intensity of flavour is much better if the drink is made entirely from rhubarb but you can also use a mixture of apple and rhubarb, if you prefer.

Lavender orange lush

This fragrant, lavender-scented juice is guaranteed to perk up a jaded palate in no time at all. Its heavenly aroma and distinct yet subtle taste is quite divine. Make plenty and keep it in the refrigerator, adding a few extra lavender sprigs to intensify the flavour, if you like. Additional sprigs make fun stirrers or a pretty garnish.

Makes 4–6 glasses

10–12 lavender flowers

45ml/3 tbsp caster (superfine) sugar

8 large oranges

ice cubes

extra lavender flowers, to serve

Pull the flowers from their stalks and put them in a bowl with the sugar and 120ml/4fl oz/½ cup boiling water. Stir until the sugar has dissolved, then leave to steep for 10 minutes.

Squeeze the oranges using a citrus juicer and pour the juice into a jug (pitcher). Strain the lavender syrup into the juice and chill.

Put a few ice cubes and a couple of lavender stirrers in glasses, top up with the juice and serve.

Fragrant fusion

Another blend of sweet and subtly flavoured fruits that packs a surprising punch. A splash of lemon and hint of fresh root ginger adds zest and bite without overpowering the delicate, fragrant flavours of lychee, cantaloupe and pear. Other types of melon can be used in place of the cantaloupe, but you will lose the pretty colour that is part of this juice's appeal.

Makes 2 tall glasses

10 lychees

1 large pear

300g/11oz wedge cantaloupe melon, rind removed

2cm/¾in piece fresh root ginger, roughly chopped

squeeze of lemon juice

crushed ice

mint sprigs, to decorate

Peel and stone (pit) the lychees and cut both the pear and the melon into large chunks.

Push the ginger, then the lychees, pear and melon through a juicer. Sharpen the flavour with a little lemon juice to taste.

Pour over crushed ice and mint sprigs in tall glasses and serve immediately.

Sweet, scented lychee and perfectly ripe cantaloupe melon shine through in this gloriously fragrant, delicately coloured blend of fresh fruits.

Peachy pleasure

When juiced together, apricots, peaches and kumquats produce the most amazingly vibrant orange-coloured juice with a flavour that has no less impact. The natural sugar content of apricots and peaches can vary enormously so you'll need to add a little honey to get the taste just right.

Makes 2 glasses

6 ripe apricots, stoned (pitted)

2 peaches, stoned (pitted)

4 kumquats

clear honey, to taste

ice cubes

Cut the apricots and peaches into large chunks and roughly chop the kumquats. Push the kumquats through a juicer, followed by the apricots and peaches.

Fill the glasses with ice cubes and pour over the juice. Serve immediately with honey.

Making decorative stirrers — Spike apricot halves on wooden skewers to make great stirrers.

Tropicana

Any blend of tropical fruits can make a fabulous juice as long as they're really ripe and ready for use. Persimmon and guavas can be quite bitter if juiced when underripe so, if necessary, leave the fruits to ripen for a few days first. The resulting juice will be well worth the wait.

Makes 2–3 glasses

1 large papaya

1 persimmon

1 large guava

juice of 2 oranges

2 passion fruit, halved

Halve the papaya, then scoop out and discard the black seeds. Cut the papaya, persimmon and guava flesh into large chunks. (There's no need to peel them.)

Push the papaya through a juicer, then do the same with the persimmon and the guava. Pour the juice into a jug (pitcher), then add the orange juice and scoop in the passion fruit pulp. Whisk and chill until ready to serve.

Black beauty

This refreshing drink celebrates the perfect partnership of blackberries and apples. The sweetness of the apples is balanced deliciously by the sharp tang and vibrant colour of the berries. Other deep red fruits such as mulberries or loganberries can be used instead of the blackberries.

Makes 2–3 tall glasses

30ml/2 tbsp golden sugar

2.5ml/½ tsp ground cinnamon

3 eating apples

200g/7oz/1¾ cups blackberries

ice cubes

borage sprigs, to decorate

Put the golden sugar in a small bowl. Add the cinnamon and 60ml/4 tbsp boiling water and stir until the sugar dissolves to form a syrup.

Roughly chop the apples. Push the blackberries through a juicer and follow with the apples. Pour in the sugar syrup and stir well to mix.

Pour the juice into tall glasses and add several ice cubes to each. Decorate the drinks with sprigs of borage or individual borage flowers, if you like, and serve immediately.

Scouring the hedgerows for perfectly ripe blackberries on a bright, clear autumn afternoon is one of life's great pleasures.

Ice cool currant

Intensely flavoured blackcurrants, whizzed in a blender with crushed ice, make a drink so thick and slushy that you might want to serve it with long spoons. If you have a glut of blackcurrants, make a double quantity of the juice and store it in the refrigerator for up to a week ready to blend with ice.

Makes 2 tall glasses

125g/4¼oz/generous 1 cup blackcurrants

60ml/4 tbsp light muscovado (brown) sugar

good pinch of mixed (apple pie) spice (optional)

225g/8oz crushed ice

Put the blackcurrants and sugar in a pan. (There is no need to string the blackcurrants first.) Add the mixed spice, if using, and pour in 100ml/3½fl oz/scant ½ cup water. Bring the mixture to the boil and cook for 2–3 minutes until the blackcurrants are completely soft.

Press the mixture through a sieve into a bowl, squeezing the pulp in with the back of a dessertspoon to extract as much juice as possible. Set aside to cool completely.

Put the crushed ice in a food processor or blender with the cooled juice and process for about 1 minute until slushy. Pour into glasses and serve immediately.

Frozen assets — This is a great juice to make if you have plenty of blackcurrants in the freezer. They'll thaw quickly as you heat them in the pan. Redcurrants or a mixture of redcurrants and blackcurrants could also be used.

Tiny, glossy blackcurrants are a virtual power-house of nutrients, packed with vitamins C and E, as well as iron, calcium and magnesium.

Energy Blends

When you're on the run and in need of a speedy food fix, a sustaining smoothie or shake can really do the trick. Whether it's a breakfast booster or stimulating snack that you're after, the blends in this chapter are guaranteed to give you a lift.

Big breakfast

Easy to prepare, and even easier to drink, this energy-packed smoothie makes a great start to any day. Bananas and sesame seeds provide the perfect fuel in the form of slow-release carbohydrate that will keep you going all morning, while fresh and zesty orange juice and sweet, scented mango will set your taste buds tingling.

Makes 2 glasses

1 banana

½ mango

1 large orange

30ml/2 tbsp wheat bran

15ml/1 tbsp sesame seeds

10–15ml/2–3 tsp honey

Peel the banana and break it into short lengths. Skin the mango, then slice the flesh off the stone (pit) and put in a food processor or blender with the banana.

Squeeze the juice from the orange and put in the food processor or blender along with the bran, sesame seeds and honey. Whizz until the mixture is smooth and creamy, then pour into glasses and serve.

Muesli smoothly

Another great breakfast booster, this store-cupboard smoothie can be a lifesaver if you've run out of fresh fruit. It's also a perfect option for breakfast in bed without the crumbs! Leftovers can be covered and stored overnight in the refrigerator, although you'll probably need to add more milk in the morning as it will undoubtedly thicken on standing.

Makes 2 tall glasses

1 piece preserved stem ginger, plus 30ml/2 tbsp syrup from the ginger jar

50g/2oz/¼ cup ready-to-eat dried apricots, halved or quartered

40g/1½oz/scant ½ cup natural muesli (granola)

200ml/7fl oz/scant 1 cup semi-skimmed (low-fat) milk

Chop the ginger and put it in a food processor or blender with the apricots, muesli and milk.

Process until smooth, adding more milk if necessary. Serve in tall glasses.

Apricot and ginger are perfect partners in this virtual dessert of a drink, which tastes absolutely divine and also makes an incredibly healthy breakfast.

Raspberry & oatmeal smoothie

Just a spoonful or so of oatmeal gives substance to this tangy, invigorating drink. If you can, prepare it ahead of time as soaking the raw oats helps to break down the starch into natural sugars that are easy to digest. The smoothie will, however, thicken up in the refrigerator so you might need to stir in a little extra juice or mineral water before serving.

Makes 1 large glass

22.5ml/1½ tbsp medium oatmeal

150g/5oz/scant 1 cup raspberries

5–10ml/1–2 tsp clear honey

45ml/3 tbsp natural (plain) yogurt

extra raspberries, to decorate

Spoon the oatmeal into a heatproof bowl. Pour in 120ml/4fl oz/½ cup boiling water and leave to stand for 10 minutes.

Put the soaked oats in a food processor or blender and add the raspberries, honey and about 30ml/2 tbsp of the yogurt. Whizz until smooth and creamy.

Pour the raspberry and oatmeal smoothie into a large glass, swirl in the remaining yogurt and top with a few extra raspberries.

Avoiding the pips — If you don't like raspberry pips (seeds), press the fruit through a sieve to make a smooth purée, then process with the oatmeal and yogurt as before. Alternatively try making the smoothie with redcurrants.

About as far from a bowl of lumpy porridge as it is possible to get, this sensuously smooth drink is a great way to enjoy wholesome oats for breakfast.

Tropical treat

Bananas are a great energy food, packed with valuable nutrients and healthy carbohydrate. Blended with additional fruits and creamy milk, this delicious concoction will keep you going for hours. Any leftover drink can be stored in the refrigerator for up to a day.

Makes 2–3 tall glasses

½ pineapple

4 Medjool dates, stoned (pitted)

1 small ripe banana

juice of 1 lemon

300ml/½ pint/1¼ cups very cold full cream (whole) milk or soya milk

Cut away the skin and core from the pineapple. Roughly chop the flesh and put it in a food processor or blender. Add the dates. Peel and chop the banana and add it to the rest of the fruit along with the lemon juice.

Blend thoroughly until smooth, stopping to scrape down the sides of the bowl with a rubber spatula if necessary.

Add the milk to the food processor or blender and process briefly until well combined. Pour the smoothie into tall glasses and serve immediately.

Zesty soya smoothie

Whizzed up with freshly squeezed orange juice, a splash of lemon and a little fragrant honey, tofu is transformed into a drink that's smooth, creamy, nutritious and delicious. Try to find silken tofu as it has a wonderfully satiny texture that blends particularly well.

Makes 1 large glass

2 oranges

15ml/1 tbsp lemon juice

20–25ml/4–5 tsp sunflower or herb honey

150g/5oz natural tofu

pared orange rind, to decorate

Finely grate the rind from the oranges and set aside. Juice the flesh using a citrus juicer and pour the juice into a food processor or blender. Add the orange rind, lemon juice, sunflower or herb honey and tofu.

Whizz the ingredients until very smooth and creamy and serve in a tall glass, decorated with pared orange rind.

Totally smooth — If you like, strain the liquid through a sieve after blending to remove the orange rind.

Mango & lime lassi

Inspired by the classic Indian drink, this tangy, fruity blend is great for breakfast or as a pick-me-up at any time of day. Soft, ripe mango blended with yogurt and sharp, zesty lime and lemon juice makes a wonderfully thick, cooling drink that's packed with energy but that can also be enjoyed as a mellow soother when you need to unwind.

Makes 2 tall glasses

1 mango

finely grated rind and juice
of 1 lime

15ml/1 tbsp lemon juice

5–10ml/1–2 tsp caster
(superfine) sugar

100ml/3½fl oz/
scant ½ cup natural
(plain) yogurt

mineral water

1 extra lime, halved,
to serve

Peel the mango and cut the flesh from the stone (pit). Put the flesh into a food processor or blender and add the lime rind and juice.

Add the lemon juice, sugar and natural yogurt. Whizz until completely smooth, scraping down the sides once or twice. Stir a little mineral water into the mixture to thin it down and create a drinkable consistency.

Serve immediately, with half a lime on the side of each glass so that more juice can be squeezed in if desired.

Choose the sweetest, juiciest mango for this exotic drink, which will remind you of warm and wonderful Indian summers.

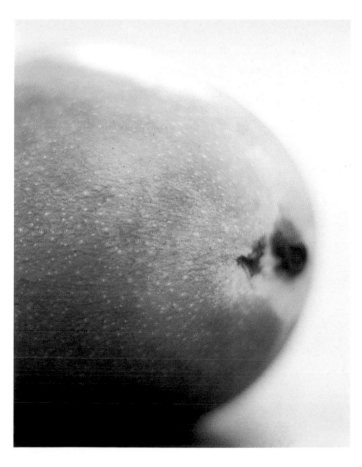

Dairy-free deluxe

Prunes, apples, oranges and soya milk may seem like an unusual combination but the results are absolutely delicious! Sweet, caramel-rich and very drinkable, this makes a great milkshake for anyone on a dairy-free diet, although regular milk can be used if you prefer.

Makes 1 tall glass

2 small eating apples

5 ready-to-eat pitted prunes

juice of 1 orange

60ml/4 tbsp soya milk

Chop, but do not peel, the apples. Push half the chopped apple through a juicer, then follow with the prunes and finish up with the remaining apples.

Pour the apple and prune juice into a jug (pitcher) and add the orange juice and soya milk. Whisk lightly until frothy. Pour into a chunky glass and serve immediately, adding a few cubes of ice, if you like.

Pear flair

For a truly refreshing combination, you can't do much better than a mixture of juicy pears and grapes. Wheatgerm adds body for a sustained energy fix and soya yogurt turns the juice into a protein-packed milkshake with a lusciously light and frothy topping.

Makes 1 large glass

1 large pear

150g/5oz/1¼ cups green grapes

15ml/1 tbsp wheatgerm

60ml/4 tbsp soya yogurt

Peel the pear and chop the flesh into large chunks. Push the chunks through a juicer with the grapes, then pour the mixture into a jug (pitcher).

Whisk the wheatgerm and yogurt into the pear and grape juice until really light and frothy. Pour the milkshake into a tall glass and serve immediately, adding a couple of ice cubes if you like your shakes to be really cold.

Very berry

Fresh and frozen cranberries are often in short supply but the dried berries are available all year round and make the most fantastically tasty dairy-free shake. This low-fat blend is packed with natural sugars, essential nutrients and valuable vitamins that are sure to give your system a hard-to-beat boost.

Makes 1 large glass

25g/1oz/¼ cup dried cranberries

150g/5oz/1¼ cups redcurrants

10ml/2 tsp clear honey

50ml/2fl oz/¼ cup soya milk

sparkling mineral water

redcurrants, to decorate

Put the cranberries in a small bowl, pour over 90ml/6 tbsp boiling water and leave to stand for 10 minutes.

String the redcurrants by drawing the stems through the tines of a fork to pull off the delicate currants.

Put the currants in a food processor or blender with the cranberries and soaking water. Blend well until smooth.

Add the clear honey and soya milk and whizz briefly to combine. Pour the shake into a large glass, top with a little sparkling mineral water and drape some redcurrants decoratively over the glass. Serve immediately.

Tiny crimson redcurrants, glistening like exquisite jewels, make the perfect partner for dark red dried cranberries in this refreshingly tart and sparkling shake.

Vital veggies

This simple blend makes a great juice boost with pure clean flavours and a chilli kick that'll revitalize flagging energy levels. Tomatoes and carrots are rich in the valuable antioxidant betacarotene, which is reputed to fight cancer, and contain a good supply of vitamins A, C and E, all of which are essential for good health.

Makes 2 glasses

250g/9oz carrots

3 tomatoes

1 fresh red or green chilli

juice of 1 orange

crushed ice

Scrub the carrots and chop them roughly. Quarter the tomatoes and roughly chop the chilli. (If you prefer a milder, less fiery juice, remove the seeds and white pith from the chilli before chopping.)

Push the carrots through a juicer, then follow with the tomatoes and chilli. Add the orange juice and stir well to mix. Fill two tumblers with crushed ice, pour over the juice and serve immediately.

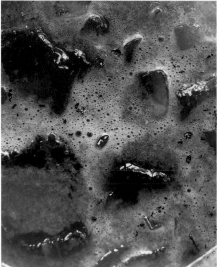

Cinnamon squash smoothie

Smoothies aren't just for fruits. Lightly cooked butternut squash has a wonderfully rich, rounded flavour that's lifted perfectly by the addition of tart citrus juice and warm, spicy cinnamon. Imagine pumpkin pie as a deliciously smooth drink and you're halfway to experiencing the flavours of this lusciously sweet and tantalizing drink.

Makes 2–3 glasses

1 small butternut squash, about 600g/1lb 6oz

2.5ml/½ tsp ground cinnamon

3 large lemons

1 grapefruit

60ml/4 tbsp light muscovado (brown) sugar

ice cubes

Halve the squash, scoop out and discard the seeds and cut the flesh into chunks. Cut away the skin and discard. Steam or boil the squash for 10–15 minutes until just tender. Drain well and set aside to cool.

Put the cooled squash in a food processor or blender and add the ground cinnamon.

Squeeze the lemons and grapefruit and pour the juice over the squash, then add the muscovado sugar.

Process the ingredients until they are very smooth. If necessary, pause to scrape down the sides of the food processor or blender.

Put a few ice cubes in two or three short glasses and pour over the smoothie. Serve immediately.

Butternut bonus — If you can only get a large squash, cook it all and add the leftovers to stew or soup.

Green devil

Choose a well-flavoured avocado, such as the knobbly dark-skinned Haas, for this melt-in-the-mouth smoothie. Cucumber adds a refreshing edge, while lemon and lime juice zip up the flavour, and the chilli sauce gives a fiery bite. This is one little devil that is sure to delight!

Makes 2–3 glasses

½ cucumber

1 small ripe avocado

30ml/2 tbsp lemon juice

30ml/2 tbsp lime juice

10ml/2 tsp caster (superfine) sugar

pinch of salt

250ml/8fl oz/1 cup apple juice or mineral water

10–20ml/2–4 tsp sweet chilli sauce

ice cubes

red chilli curls, to decorate

Peel and roughly chop the cucumber and put in a food processor or blender. Halve the avocado and use a sharp knife to remove the stone (pit). Scoop the flesh from both halves into the food processor or blender and add the lemon and lime juice, caster sugar and salt.

Process until smooth and creamy, then add the apple juice or water and a little of the chilli sauce. Blend lightly to mix.

Put ice cubes in glasses and pour over the smoothie. Decorate with red chilli curls and serve with stirrers and extra chilli sauce for stirring in.

Chilli curls — To make chilli curls, core and seed a fresh red chilli and cut into very fine strips. Put in a bowl of iced water and leave for at least 20 minutes until the strips curl.

Seductively smooth avocados are as good for you as they taste. Their fresh vitamin- and mineral-rich flesh is reputed to be great for healthy hair and skin.

Smooth & Creamy

Fabulously indulgent pure fruit mixes, creamy creations and icy slushes are the ultimate in comfort blending. Whether they're rich and luscious or sweet and refreshing, these smooth-as-silk drinks are really worth taking your time over.

Ruby dreamer

Figs have a distinctive yet delicate taste and are best used in simple combinations, with ingredients that enhance, rather than mask, their flavour. Like most fruits, fresh figs are now available most of the year round but they are often at their best in winter when ruby oranges are also in season – giving you the perfect excuse to make this veritable treat of a smoothie.

Makes 2 glasses

6 large ripe figs

4 ruby oranges

15ml/1 tbsp dark muscovado (brown) sugar

30–45ml/2–3 tbsp lemon juice

Cut off the hard, woody tips from the stalks of the figs, then use a sharp knife to cut each fruit in half.

Squeeze the oranges, using a citrus juicer or by hand. Pour the juice into a food processor or blender and add the figs and sugar. Process well until the mixture is really smooth and fairly thick, scraping the fruit down from the sides of the bowl if necessary.

Add lemon juice to taste and blend briefly to mix. Pour into glasses and serve.

Thyme-scented plum lush

Make this divine drink in the early autumn when plums tend to be at their sweetest and best. Their silky smooth flesh blends down to produce the most wonderfully textured smoothie, while delicately scented lemon thyme and honey complement the flavour perfectly. It is easy to make and has an irresistible fragrance that is at once warming and refreshing.

Makes 2–3 glasses

400g/14oz red plums

30–45ml/2–3 tbsp clear honey

15ml/1 tbsp chopped fresh lemon thyme

100g/3¾oz crushed ice

extra thyme leaves, to decorate

Halve and stone (pit) the plums and put in a food processor or blender. Add 30ml/2 tbsp of the honey and the lemon thyme and blend until smooth, scraping down the sides of the bowl if necessary.

Add the ice and blend until slushy. Taste for sweetness, adding a little more honey if necessary. Pour into glasses and serve immediately with a few thyme leaves.

Dark purplish-red plums, with their almost violet bloom and sweet, intense flavour, make one of the most tempting and vibrant fruit drinks.

Rosemary nectar

This is one of those smoothies that's only worth making if you've got the perfect ingredients. You need really plump, sweet and juicy nectarines, bursting with flavour and colour. If you've bought nectarines only to find that they're as hard as bullets, leave them in the fruit bowl for a couple of days and they should ripen fairly quickly.

Makes 3 glasses

4 long rosemary sprigs

15ml/1 tbsp golden caster (superfine) sugar

2.5ml/½ tsp ground ginger

2 oranges

4 nectarines

ice cubes

extra long rosemary sprigs

Put the rosemary sprigs in a small pan with the sugar, ginger and 150ml/¼ pint/ ⅔ cup water. Heat gently until the sugar dissolves, then simmer for 1 minute. Remove from the heat, transfer the sprigs and syrup to a bowl and leave to cool.

Squeeze the oranges. Halve and stone (pit) the nectarines and put in a food processor or blender with the orange juice. Process until smooth but don't worry if there are a few specks of the nectarine skin dotting the juice.

Remove the rosemary sprigs from the syrup and pour the syrup into the juice. Blend briefly to combine.

Put a few ice cubes and a couple of long rosemary sprigs in each glass and fill with the juice. Serve immediately.

The fabulously aromatic fragrance of rosemary reacts with the sweet, scented flavour of ripe nectarines to produce a smoothie whose taste practically explodes on the tongue.

Rhubarb & allspice cream

Make this delicious blend early in the season, when rhubarb is young, pink and tender. If you leave it until later in the year, the stalks will be tougher, possibly stringy, and so acidic that you'll need heaps of sugar to make the juice the indulgent treat that it should be. Make sure you serve with a spoon to scoop up every last dribble – you won't want to leave a drop!

Makes 4 glasses

500g/1¼lb early rhubarb

100ml/3½fl oz/
scant ½ cup freshly
squeezed orange juice

75g/3oz/scant ½ cup
caster (superfine) sugar

2.5ml/½ tsp ground
allspice

100ml/3½fl oz/scant ½ cup
double (heavy) cream

200ml/7fl oz/scant 1 cup
full cream (whole) milk

crushed ice

Trim the rhubarb and cut it into chunks. Put in a pan with the orange juice, sugar and allspice and bring to the boil. Cover and simmer gently for 6–8 minutes until tender. Remove from the heat and leave to cool.

Transfer the rhubarb and cooking juice to a food processor or blender and process in short bursts until smooth, scraping down the sides if necessary.

Add the cream and milk to the rhubarb purée and blend again until combined. Transfer to a jug (pitcher) and chill until ready to serve.

Half-fill glasses with crushed ice, pour over the juice and serve immediately.

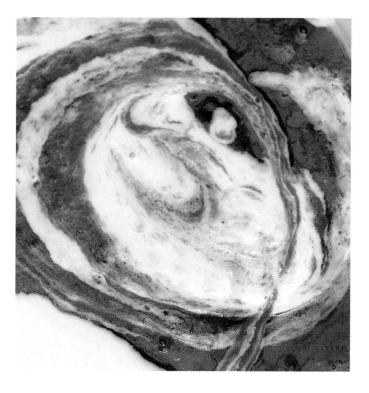

Pale shoots of young rhubarb, poached with sugar and spice, and blended with cream, make a truly dreamy concoction that's just too tempting to turn down.

Frosty fruits

Long after summer is over you can still summon up those glorious flavours by making this fruity and refreshing drink from frozen summer fruits. It takes only moments to whizz up and you can use any mixture of fruits, whether you've grown and frozen your own berries or bought them in bags from the frozen food section of the supermarket.

Makes 2–3 glasses

250g/9oz frozen summer fruits, such as strawberries, raspberries, blackberries, blackcurrants or redcurrants

200g/7oz/scant 1 cup natural (plain) yogurt

45ml/3 tbsp double (heavy) cream

30–45ml/2–3 tbsp caster (superfine) sugar

Take the fruits straight from the freezer and tip them into a food processor or blender. Blend until finely crushed, scraping down the sides of the bowl if necessary.

Add the yogurt and cream to the crushed fruit, then spoon in 30ml/2 tbsp of the sugar. Blend again until the mixture is smooth and thick. Taste and add the extra sugar if necessary. Serve immediately.

Mango mania

Even those on a dairy-free diet can enjoy the richest, creamiest most indulgent drinks. This one's made using soya milk, which is particularly good in milkshakes and smoothies. It has a lovely caramel flavour that blends very well with fruit purées, especially those based on fruits with a sweet, intense taste such as apricots or mangoes.

Makes 2 tall glasses

1 medium mango

300ml/½ pint/1¼ cups soya milk

finely grated rind and juice of 1 lime, plus 15ml/1 tbsp extra juice

15–30ml/1–2 tbsp clear honey

Peel the mango and cut the flesh off the stone (pit). Place the chopped flesh in a food processor or blender, and add the soya milk, lime rind and juice and a little honey. Blend until smooth and frothy.

Taste the mixture and add a little more honey, if necessary. Whizz again until well mixed, then pour over crushed ice in tall glasses.

Sugar fix— for those with a sweet tooth, choose soya milk sweetened with apple juice for this recipe. It's readily available in supermarkets and has a really rich flavour.

The heady, scented aroma of mangoes and the buttery texture of their flesh makes them the perfect choice for smooth-as-silk blended drinks.

Purple haze

Thick, dark purple blueberry purée swirled into pale and creamy vanilla-flavoured buttermilk looks stunning and tastes simply divine. Despite its creaminess, the buttermilk gives this sumptuous smoothie a delicious tang. If you can't find buttermilk in the supermarket, you can use a mixture of half yogurt and half milk instead.

Makes 2 tall glasses

250g/9oz/2¼ cups blueberries

50g/2oz/¼ cup caster (superfine) sugar

15ml/1 tbsp lemon juice

300ml/½ pint/1¼ cups buttermilk

5ml/1 tsp vanilla essence (extract)

150ml/¼ pint/⅔ cup full cream (whole) milk

Push the blueberries through the juicer and stir in 15ml/1 tbsp of the sugar and the lemon juice. Stir well and divide between two tall glasses.

Put the buttermilk, vanilla essence, milk and remaining sugar in a food processor or blender and process until really frothy. (Alternatively use a hand-held electric blender and blend until the mixture froths up.)

Pour the buttermilk mixture over the blueberry juice, so the mixtures swirl together, and serve immediately.

Pure, creamy buttermilk threaded with streams of richly flavoured, deep violet blueberry juice creates a stupendous, smooth and syrupy smoothie.

Rose petal & almond milk

If you're lucky enough to have a mass of roses in the garden, it's well worth sacrificing a few to this delicately scented summer smoothie. Thickened and flavoured with ground ratafia biscuits, this fragrant drink is the perfect way to relax on a hot summer's afternoon.

Makes 2 glasses

15g/½oz scented rose petals (preferably pink)

300ml/½ pint/1¼ cups milk

25g/1oz ratafia biscuits (almond macaroons)

ice cubes

Put the rose petals in a small pan with half the milk and bring just to the boil. Put the biscuits in a bowl, pour over the hot milk and leave to stand for 10 minutes.

Transfer the mixture to a food processor or blender with the remaining milk and process until smooth.

Strain the milk through a sieve and chill for at least 1 hour. Serve over ice cubes in tumblers.

Banana, pecan nut & maple smoothie

Bananas are a brilliant fruit for making quick and easy blended drinks, and they have a natural affinity with maple syrup and pecan nuts. Serve this scrumptious smoothie over ice as soon as it is ready, as it won't keep well.

Makes 2 glasses

50g/2oz/½ cup pecan nuts

2 large bananas

150ml/¼ pint/⅔ cup full cream (whole) milk

60ml/4 tbsp pure maple syrup

crushed ice

Put the pecan nuts in a food processor or blender and process until finely chopped. Add the bananas and blend again to make a thick, smooth paste. The nuts must be very finely ground so stop and scrape down the sides of the bowl once or twice if necessary.

Pour the milk over the banana paste, add the maple syrup and blend until smooth and creamy. Half-fill glasses with crushed ice and pour the smoothie over the top. Pop a stirrer in each glass, if you like, and serve immediately.

Vanilla snow

While a good quality vanilla essence is perfectly acceptable for desserts and baking, a far better result will be achieved by using a vanilla pod. This simple smoothie is deliciously scented, creamy and thick, and well worth the extravagance of using a whole vanilla pod. Its lovely snowy whiteness is delightfully speckled with tiny black vanilla seeds.

Makes 3 glasses

1 vanilla pod (bean)

25g/1oz/2 tbsp caster (superfine) sugar

3 eating apples

300g/11oz/1⅓ cups natural (plain) yogurt

Using the tip of a sharp knife, split open the vanilla pod lengthways. Put it in a small pan with the sugar and 75ml/5 tbsp water. Heat until the sugar dissolves, then boil for 1 minute. Remove from the heat and leave to steep for 10 minutes.

Cut the apples into large chunks and push through the juicer, then pour the juice to a large bowl or jug (pitcher).

Lift the vanilla pod out of the pan and scrape the tiny black seeds back into the syrup. Pour the syrup into the apple juice.

Add the yogurt to the bowl or jug and whisk well by hand or with an electric mixer until the smoothie is thick and frothy. Pour into glasses and serve.

Chill out — Like most smoothies this one needs to be served well chilled. Either use apples and yogurt straight from the refrigerator, or chill briefly before serving. To make a thick, icy version, you could use frozen yogurt.

Eastern essence

While juicing the flesh from a whole fresh coconut makes the purest form of coconut milk, canned milk makes a good substitute and gives excellent results. Aromatic lemon grass gives an exotic edge to this delicately flavoured drink. To enjoy it at its best, remember to chill the coconut milk for a couple of hours before you start.

Makes 3 glasses

2 lemon grass stalks

150ml/¼ pint/⅔ cup full cream (whole) milk

40g/1½oz/3 tbsp caster (superfine) sugar

400ml/14fl oz can coconut milk, chilled

120ml/4fl oz/½ cup single (light) cream

crushed ice

Halve the lemon grass stalks lengthways and bruise them by pounding with the end of a rolling pin. Put the lemon grass in a pan, pour over the milk and bring to the boil. Remove from the heat and leave to steep for 20 minutes.

Strain the milk through a sieve into a food processor or blender and add the sugar, coconut milk and cream.

Process the mixture until thoroughly blended and frothy. Half-fill glasses with crushed ice, pour the smoothie over the top and serve immediately.

The Thai-inspired flavours of coconut and lemon grass marry beautifully in this rich and fragrant smoothie, which has a subtle taste of the Far East.

Garden mint milkshake

If you have mint growing in your garden, pick it for this recipe as the fresher the mint, the better the flavour will be. It's infused in a sugar syrup, then left to cool before being blended to an aromatic, frothy shake with yogurt and creamy milk. The final milkshake is speckled with tiny flecks of mint, but if you prefer a completely smooth texture, you can leave these out.

Makes 2 tall glasses

25g/1oz/1 cup fresh mint

50g/2oz/¼ cup caster (superfine) sugar

200g/7oz/scant 1 cup natural (plain) yogurt

200ml/7fl oz/scant 1 cup full cream (whole) milk

15ml/1 tbsp lemon juice

crushed ice cubes

mint sprigs and icing (confectioners') sugar, to decorate

Pull out four mint sprigs and set aside. Roughly snip the remaining leaves into a small pan. Add the sugar and pour over 105ml/7 tbsp water.

Heat the mixture, stirring occasionally, until the sugar dissolves, then boil for 2 minutes. Remove the pan from the heat and set aside until the syrup is completely cool.

Strain the cooled syrup through a sieve into a jug (pitcher), pressing the mint against the side of the sieve with the back of a spoon to extract all the syrup. Pour into a food processor or blender.

Add the yogurt and milk to the syrup and blend until smooth and frothy. Add two of the reserved mint sprigs and lemon juice and blend until the milkshake is specked with tiny green flecks.

Put the crushed ice in tall glasses or tumblers and pour over the milkshake. Dust the mint sprigs with icing sugar and decorate the glasses.

Dessert Drinks

These utterly irresistible blends make you wonder when the dessert stops and a drink starts. Classic combinations such as blueberry and meringue, strawberry and marshmallow, and banana and toffee are brought together to create the sweetest, stickiest, most luscious of smoothies and shakes.

Candystripe

This wickedly indulgent drink combines freshly blended strawberries with a marshmallow flavoured cream, making a milkshake that adults as well as kids will find totally irresistible. If you can keep family and friends away from it for long enough, the drink will benefit from being chilled for an hour or so before being served.

Makes 4 tall glasses

150g/5oz white and pink marshmallows

500ml/17fl oz/generous 2 cups full cream (whole) milk

60ml/4 tbsp redcurrant jelly

450g/1lb/4 cups strawberries

60ml/4 tbsp double (heavy) cream

extra strawberries and marshmallows, to decorate

Put the marshmallows in a heavy pan with half the milk and heat gently, stirring frequently, until the marshmallows have melted. Set aside to cool.

Heat the redcurrant jelly in a small pan until melted. Put the strawberries in a food processor or blender and process until smooth, scraping down the sides of the bowl as often as is necessary.

Stir 10ml/2 tsp of the strawberry purée into the melted jelly. Pour the remaining purée into a jug (pitcher) and add the marshmallow mixture, cream and the remaining milk. Chill the milkshake and four empty tall glasses for about 1 hour.

To serve, use a teaspoon to drizzle lines of the redcurrant syrup down the insides of the glasses – this creates a candystripe effect when filled. Fill the glasses with the milkshake. Serve topped with the extra marshmallows and strawberries and drizzle with any leftover strawberry syrup.

There's no point in trying to resist the melting marshmallow sweetness of this cheeky little strawberry confection – just sit back and give yourself up!

Blueberry meringue crumble

Imagine the most appealing flavours of a blueberry meringue dessert – fresh tangy fruit, crisp sugary meringue and plenty of vanilla-scented cream. This drink combines all those flavours in one delicious milkshake. Iced yogurt provides a slightly lighter note than ice cream but there's nothing to stop you using ice cream instead for an even greater indulgence.

Makes 3–4 tall glasses

150g/5oz/1¼ cups fresh blueberries

15ml/1 tbsp icing (confectioners') sugar

250ml/8fl oz/1 cup vanilla or citrus iced yogurt

200ml/7fl oz/scant 1 cup full cream (whole) milk

30ml/2 tbsp lime juice

75g/3oz meringues, lightly crushed

extra blueberries, to decorate (optional)

Put the blueberries and sugar in a food processor or blender with 60ml/4 tbsp water and blend until smooth, scraping the mixture down from the sides once or twice if necessary.

Transfer the purée to a small bowl and rinse out the food processor bowl or blender jug to get rid of any of the blueberry juice.

Put the iced yogurt, milk and lime juice in the food processor or blender and process until combined. Add half the crushed meringues and blend until smooth.

Pour alternate layers of the milkshake, blueberry syrup and the remaining crushed meringues into tall glasses, finishing with a few chunky pieces of meringue and drizzling over any remaining blueberry syrup. Top with extra blueberries, if using.

To crush meringues — The easiest way to crush the meringues is to put them in a plastic bag on the work surface and tap gently with a rolling pin. Stop tapping the meringues as soon as they have crumbled into bitesize pieces.

Rum & raisin thick-shake

This milkshake is remarkably easy to prepare, and vastly superior to any store-bought rum and raisin concoction. Use a good quality ice cream, leave it to soften slightly in the refrigerator before scooping, and you simply can't go wrong. If the raisins are a little dry, then leave them to soak in the rum for a few minutes to soften and plump up before you blend them.

Makes 2 tall glasses

75g/3oz/generous ½ cup raisins

45ml/3 tbsp dark rum

300ml/ ½ pint/1¼ cups full cream (whole) milk

500ml/17fl oz/2¼ cups good quality vanilla ice cream

Put the raisins, rum and a little of the milk into a food processor or blender and process for about 1 minute, or until the raisins are finely chopped.

Spoon two large scoops of the vanilla ice cream into two tall glasses, then put the remaining ice cream and milk into the food processor or blender and blend until creamy.

Pour the shake into the glasses and serve immediately with straws and long spoons for scooping up the chunks of raisin that collect in the base of each glass.

Foaming citrus eggnog

For most of us, eggnog is inextricably associated with the festive season. This version, however, pepped up with orange rind and juice for a lighter, fresher taste, has a much wider appeal. Whether you sip it as a late-night soother, serve it as a wintry dessert or enjoy it as cosy tipple on a wet afternoon, it's sure to bring a warm, rosy glow to your cheeks.

Makes 2 glasses

2 small oranges

150ml/ ¼ pint/ ⅔ cup single (light) cream

plenty of freshly grated nutmeg

2.5ml/ ½ tsp ground cinnamon

2.5ml/ ½ tsp cornflour (cornstarch)

2 eggs, separated

30ml/2 tbsp light muscovado (brown) sugar

45ml/3 tbsp brandy

Finely grate the rind from the oranges, then squeeze out the juice and pour it into a jug (pitcher).

Put the rind in a small heavy pan with the cream, nutmeg, cinnamon and cornflour. Heat gently over a low heat, stirring frequently until bubbling.

Meanwhile, put the egg yolks in a bowl and whisk with the sugar, using a hand-held electric mixer.

Stir the hot citrus cream mixture into the egg yolks, then return to the pan. Pour in the orange juice and brandy and heat very gently, stirring until slightly thickened.

Whisk the egg whites in a large, clean bowl until foamy and light.

Strain the cream mixture through a sieve into the whisked whites. Stir gently and pour into heatproof punch cups, handled glasses or mugs. If you like, sprinkle over a little extra nutmeg before serving.

This warm, zesty citrus eggnog, with its light-as-air consistency, calls to mind a sippable citrus zabaglione.

Banoffee high

You may as well make plenty of this outrageous, lip-smacking milkshake because everyone will love it. If you use a blender, make sure it is powerful enough to cope with ice cubes. If you have time, make the syrup a little in advance so it can thicken, and keep any leftovers in the refrigerator to use as a quick toffee sauce for spooning over ice cream.

Makes 4 tall glasses

75g/3oz/ ½ cup light muscovado (brown) sugar

150ml/ ¼ pint/ ²⁄₃ cup double (heavy) cream

4 large bananas

600ml/1 pint/2½ cups full cream (whole) milk

15ml/1 tbsp vanilla sugar

8 ice cubes

To make the toffee syrup, put the sugar in a small heavy pan with 75ml/5 tbsp water. Cook gently, stirring until the sugar dissolves, then add 45ml/3 tbsp of the cream and bring to the boil. Let the syrup simmer for about 4 minutes until thickened. Remove from the heat and leave to cool for 30 minutes.

Peel the bananas, break into pieces and put into a food processor or blender with the milk, vanilla sugar, ice cubes and a further 45ml/3 tbsp of the cream. Process until smooth and frothy.

Pour the remaining cream into a bowl and whip lightly with a whisk or hand-held electric mixer until it just holds its shape.

Add half the toffee syrup to the milkshake and blend to combine, then pour into glasses. Drizzle more syrup around the insides of the glasses to create a marbled effect. Spoon over the whipped cream and drizzle with any remaining syrup.

Nobody is pretending this wild extravagance is a health drink, but you're guaranteed an energy rush of astronomic proportions!

Coconut ice

Nothing beats the unadulterated, pure flavour of freshly juiced coconut. Whizzed with plenty of crushed ice and teamed with sharp, intensely flavoured passion fruit, it produces a milkshake that tastes indulgently good but still refreshingly natural and wholesome.

Makes 2–3 glasses

1 coconut

75ml/5 tbsp icing (confectioners') sugar

3 passion fruit

150g/5oz crushed ice

60ml/4 tbsp double (heavy) cream

Drain the milk from the coconut and reserve. Break open the coconut, remove the flesh, then peel off the brown skin. Push the coconut pieces through a juicer along with 150ml/¼ pint/²⁄₃ cup water. Stir the icing sugar into the coconut juice and set aside.

Halve the passion fruit and, using a teaspoon, scoop the pulp into a small bowl. Set aside.

Put the crushed ice in a food processor or blender and process until slushy. Add the juiced coconut, any drained coconut milk and the cream. Process just long enough to blend the ingredients.

Pour the mixture into tall stemmed glasses, then, using a teaspoon, spoon the passion fruit on top of the drink. Add stirrers, if you like, and serve immediately.

Death by chocolate

There are only two ingredients used in this decadently rich smoothie: creamy milk and the best chocolate you can buy. Blended together, they make the smoothest, frothiest and most chocolatey drink you will ever taste. Once tried, you will never view a chocolate smoothie in the same light again.

Makes 2 large glasses

150g/5oz good quality chocolate

350ml/12fl oz/1½ cups full cream (whole) milk

ice cubes

chocolate curls or shavings, to serve

Break the chocolate into pieces and place in a bowl set over a pan of simmering water. Add 60ml/4 tbsp of the milk and leave until the chocolate melts, stirring occasionally.

Remove the bowl from the heat and pour the remaining milk over the chocolate, stirring to combine.

Pour the mixture into a food processor or blender and blend until smooth and frothy. Pour into glasses, add ice cubes and serve, topped with the chocolate decoration.

Chocolate choice — Depending on personal taste, use dark (bittersweet) chocolate with 70 per cent cocoa solids, or a good quality milk chocolate. If you like the intensity of dark chocolate but the creaminess of milk, use half of each.

Turkish delight

Lovers of Turkish delight beware! This drink is totally addictive and couldn't be easier to make. With the scented aroma of rose water and the icy sweetness of vanilla ice cream, it's hard to imagine a more decadent combination of ingredients.

Makes 3–4 glasses

125g/4¼oz rose-flavoured Turkish delight

475ml/16fl oz/2 cups semi-skimmed (low-fat) milk

250ml/8fl oz/1 cup good quality vanilla ice cream

a little finely grated plain (semisweet) chocolate, or drinking chocolate powder, for sprinkling (optional)

Roughly chop the Turkish delight, or snip up with scissors if easier. Reserve a few pieces for decoration and put the rest in a pan with half the milk. Heat gently until the pieces have begun to melt. Remove from the heat and leave to cool.

Scrape the mixture into a food processor or blender and add the remaining milk. Process until smooth, then add the ice cream and blend briefly to combine.

Pour into glasses, top with the reserved Turkish delight and serve with a sprinkle of chocolate or drinking chocolate powder to decorate, if liked.

Extra froth — For an even frothier top, pour the milkshake into a large bowl and whizz with a hand-held electric mixer.

Rich and milky, sweet and exceedingly silky, this smooth, creamy drink is perhaps the ultimate indulgence.

Nutty nougat

For the best results, chill this glorious milkshake for a few hours until it is icy cold and the jumble of ingredients have had time to merge and meld into a hedonistic fusion of flavours. Skinning the pistachio nuts is not essential, but it makes a fabulous visual impact, transforming the specks of nut from a dull green to a vivid emerald colour.

Makes 3 glasses

90ml/6 tbsp sweetened condensed milk

300ml/½ pint/1¼ cups semi-skimmed (low-fat) milk

100ml/3½fl oz/scant ½ cup crème fraîche

15ml/1 tbsp lemon juice

25g/1oz/¼ cup skinned pistachio nuts

25g/1oz/¼ cup blanched almonds

25g/1oz/3 tbsp candied peel, finely chopped, plus a few extra slices for decoration

ice cubes

Put the condensed milk and the semi-skimmed milk in a food processor or blender. Add the crème fraîche and blend until combined.

Add the lemon juice, pistachio nuts, almonds and chopped peel to the food processor or blender and process until chopped into tiny pieces. Pour over ice cubes in tall glasses, add a few slices of candied peel and serve immediately.

Skinning pistachio nuts — To skin the nuts, put them in a heatproof bowl, cover with boiling water and leave for 2 minutes. Drain and rub between layers of kitchen paper to loosen the skins. Pick out the nuts, peeling off remaining skin.

Pretty, emerald-green flecks of pistachio nut pepper the rich, nougat-flavoured milkshake, giving it the subtlest colour and the most wonderful texture.

Sparkling peach melba

Serve this liquid version of the classic dessert during the summer months when raspberries and peaches are at their sweetest and best. Traditional cream soda gives this drink a really smooth flavour and a lovely fizz, while the optional shot of Drambuie or brandy gives it a certain kick. Serve with long spoons for scooping up any fruit left in the glasses.

Makes 2 glasses

300g/11oz/scant 2 cups raspberries

2 large ripe peaches

30ml/2 tbsp Drambuie or brandy (optional)

15ml/1 tbsp icing (confectioners') sugar

cream soda

Pack a few raspberries into six tiny shot glasses, or into six sections of an ice cube tray, and pour over water to cover. Freeze for several hours.

Halve and stone (pit) the peaches and cut one half into thin slices. Reserve 115g/4oz/ ^{2}/$_3$ cup of the raspberries and divide the rest, along with the peach slices, between two tall stemmed glasses. Drizzle with the liqueur, if using.

Push the reserved raspberries and the remaining peach flesh through the juicer. Stir the icing sugar into the juice and pour over the fruits.

Turn the raspberry-filled ice cubes out of the shot glasses or ice cube tray and add three to each glass. Top up with cream soda and serve immediately.

Soft, rounded raspberries and juicy peach slices bob flirtatiously among the nose-tingling bubbles of this delightful, icy sparkler.

Lemon float

Old-fashioned lemonade made with freshly squeezed lemons is a far cry from the carbonated synthetic commercial varieties. Served with generous scoops of ice cream and soda water it makes the ultimate in refreshing dessert drinks. The lemonade can be stored in the refrigerator for up to two weeks so it's well worth making a double batch.

Makes 4 large glasses

6 lemons

200g/7oz/1 cup caster (superfine) sugar

8 scoops vanilla ice cream

soda water (club soda)

lemon, cut into wafer thin slices, to decorate

Finely grate the rind from the lemons, then squeeze out the juice using a citrus juicer or by hand.

Put the rind in a bowl with the sugar and pour over 600ml/1 pint/2½ cups boiling water. Stir until the sugar dissolves, then leave to cool.

Stir in the lemon juice. Strain into a jug (pitcher) and chill for several hours.

Put a scoop of ice cream in each glass, then half-fill with the lemonade and add plenty of lemon slices. Top up with soda water and add another scoop of ice cream to each glass and serve immediately.

What could be more delectable than the sharp, zesty zing of lemon contrasted with the sweet creaminess of ice cream?

120 Dessert Drinks

Super sorbet fizz

Freshly blended pineapple and lemon sorbet, topped up with ginger ale, makes a tastebud-tingling drink. Perfect after a summer lunch as a light alternative to more conventional desserts, or one to whizz up and chill out with whenever the mood takes you.

Makes 4 glasses

30ml/2 tbsp dark muscovado (brown) sugar

15ml/1 tbsp lemon juice

½ pineapple

1 piece preserved stem ginger, roughly chopped

200ml/7fl oz/scant 1 cup lemon sorbet, slightly softened

ginger ale, chilled

wafer thin pineapple and lemon slices, to decorate

Mix the sugar with the lemon juice in a small bowl and leave to stand for about 5 minutes until it turns syrupy.

Discard the skin and core from the pineapple and cut the flesh into chunks. Put the chunks in a food processor or blender with the ginger and whizz until smooth, scraping down the sides of the bowl once or twice if necessary.

Add the sorbet and blend briefly until smooth. Spoon the muscovado syrup into four tumblers, then pour in the pineapple mixture.

Decorate the sides of the glasses with the pineapple and lemon slices. Top up with ginger ale and serve immediately.

Canning it— If you're in a hurry, you can use canned pineapple but the flavour won't be as fresh or intense.

Fresh pineapple blended with tangy lemon sorbet and topped with ice cold sparkling ginger ale virtually explodes on the tongue in a symphony of flavours in this gorgeous semi-frozen blend.

Party Pieces

From creamy cocktails to fruity punches and juicy shots, blending and juicing are the way forward when it comes to creating the perfect party brew. This fabulous selection of refreshing spritzers, punch-packing cocktails and teetotal tipples are guaranteed to get your gathering in full swing.

Pineapple & coconut rum crush

This thick and slushy tropical cooler is unbelievably rich thanks to the combination of coconut milk and thick cream. The addition of sweet, juicy and slightly tart pineapple and finely crushed ice offers a refreshing foil, making it all too easy to sip your way through several glasses.

Makes 4–5 large glasses

1 pineapple

30ml/2 tbsp lemon juice

200ml/7fl oz/scant 1 cup coconut milk

150ml/¼ pint/⅔ cup double (heavy) cream

200ml/7fl oz/scant 1 cup white rum

30–60ml/2–4 tbsp caster (superfine) sugar

500g/1¼lb finely crushed ice

Trim off the ends from the pineapple, then remove the skin. Cut away the core and chop the flesh. Put the chopped flesh in a food processor or blender with the lemon juice and whizz until very smooth.

Add the coconut milk, cream, rum and 30ml/2 tbsp of the sugar to the pineapple. Blend until thoroughly combined, then taste and add more sugar if necessary.

Pack the ice into glasses, add straws, if you like, and pour over the drink. Serve immediately.

Time saver — This is a great cocktail for making ahead of time. Blend the drink in advance and chill in a jug (pitcher). Store the crushed ice in the freezer ready for serving as soon as it's required.

Rather like a thick and creamy pina colada cocktail, this luxuriously rich tropical blend offers a hefty rum-kick and is likely to satisfy your appetite for hours!

Tropical fruit royale

This recipe is a fresh and fruity variation on a kir royale, in which champagne is poured over crème de cassis. Made with tropical fruits and sparkling wine, it can work out cheaper than the champagne version but still has a wonderfully elegant feel. Remember to blend the fruits ahead of time to give the mango ice cubes time to freeze.

Makes 6 glasses

2 large mangoes

6 passion fruit

sparkling wine

Peel the mangoes, cut the flesh off the stone (pit), then put the flesh in a food processor or blender. Process until smooth, scraping the mixture down from the sides of the bowl.

Fill an ice cube tray with a good half of the purée and freeze for 2 hours.

Cut six wedges from one or two of the passion fruits and scoop the pulp from the rest of the passion fruits into the remaining mango purée. Process until well blended.

Spoon the mixture into six stemmed glasses. Divide the mango ice cubes among the glasses, top up with sparkling wine and add the passion fruit wedges. Serve with stirrers.

Delight your guests with this delicious thirst-quencher. With its taste of the tropics, it makes the perfect choice on a balmy summer evening.

Apple-tice

Even the dullest of eating apples seem to juice well. With the addition of a fresh mint syrup and sparkling cider, the plainest juice can be transformed into a distinctly exciting, mildly alcoholic blend that makes an excellent party drink. Because you can choose how much cider you add, it's easy to control your alcohol consumption.

Makes 6–8 glasses

25g/1oz/1 cup mint leaves

15g/½oz/1 tbsp caster (superfine) sugar

6 eating apples

ice cubes

mint sprigs

1 litre/1¾ pints/4 cups dry (hard) cider

Roughly snip the mint into a heatproof jug (pitcher). Add the sugar, then pour over 200ml/7fl oz/scant 1 cup boiling water. Stir until the sugar dissolves, then set aside to cool.

Chop the apples into chunks and push through a juicer. Drain the mint from the syrup and discard. Mix the apple juice and syrup in a large jug and chill until ready to serve.

To serve, add ice cubes and mint sprigs and top up with cider.

Crisp, juicy apples, fresh, cooling mint and sparkling dry cider are perfect partners in this fabulously fruity tipple that is guaranteed to appeal to everyone.

Iced strawberry daiquiri

The classic daiquiri cocktail is named after a village in Cuba that lies near the Barcardi processing plant. The original version was an incredibly potent blend of rum and whisky but the fruit versions, which are so popluar today, are slightly less alcoholic. To make a banana version of this drink, simply replace the strawberries with two bananas.

Makes 4 small glasses

4 limes

60ml/4 tbsp icing (confectioners') sugar

200ml/7fl oz/scant 1 cup white rum

275g/10oz/2½ cups strawberries

300g/10oz crushed ice

Squeeze the limes, using a citrus juicer or by hand and pour the juice into a food processor or blender. Add the icing sugar, rum and strawberries and process until really smooth and frothy.

Add the crushed ice to the food processor or blender and process again until slushy. Pour into glasses and serve immediately.

Extra icy— To make a really slushy, thick iced daiquiri, use frozen strawberries. There's no need to leave them to thaw, just use them as they are.

Blushing pink and icy cool, this sweetly sumptuous boozy blend is guaranteed to bring a smile to your lips and put a sparkle in your eye.

Frozen margarita

For the serious cocktail connoisseur, the margarita sipped from the salt-crusted rim of a glass is simply the best. A classic citrus juicer will help you to get the maximum juice from limes, but if the fruits are very firm and don't yield much juice, try microwaving them briefly first.

Makes 8 small glasses

150ml/¼ pint/⅔ cup lime juice, from about 6 large limes

sea salt flakes

120ml/4fl oz/½ cup cointreau or grand marnier

200ml/7fl oz/ scant 1 cup tequila

150g/5oz crushed ice

1 lime, thinly sliced, to decorate

To coat the glass rims with salt, put 30ml/2 tbsp of the lime juice into a saucer and plenty of salt flakes in another. Turn the glasses upside down and dip the rim of each glass in the lime juice, then in the salt. Invert again and set aside.

Put the remaining lime juice in a food processor or blender with the cointreau or grand marnier, tequila and crushed ice. Process until the mixture is slushy.

Pour the margarita mixture into the salt-rimmed glasses, add a slice or two of lime to each glass and serve immediately.

Sharp and sassy lime juice, tongue-tingling tequila, and sweet and smooth cointreau meld perfectly to make this classic cocktail a sure-fire success at any party.

Raspberry rendezvous

Pink, raspberry-flavoured bubbles and a suspicion of brandy makes this the ultimate in sippable sophistication. A splash of sweet, sugary grenadine added to the jewel-coloured raspberry juice will smooth out any hint of a sharp tang that there might be from slightly underripe fruit.

Makes 6 glasses

400g/14oz/2⅓ cups raspberries

100ml/3½fl oz/scant ½ cup grenadine

100ml/3½fl oz/scant ½ cup brandy or cherry brandy

ice cubes

extra raspberries (optional)

1 litre/1¾ pints/4 cups ginger ale, chilled

Push the raspberries through a juicer and pour the juice into a jug (pitcher).

Stir the grenadine and brandy or cherry brandy into the juice and chill until ready to serve.

To serve, pour the raspberry mixture into six tall glasses, add a few ice cubes and extra raspberries, if using, then top up with chilled ginger ale.

Grenadine — This intensely sweet, ruby-coloured syrup is made from pomegranates and is popularly used to enhance fruit juices and cocktails. True grenadine contains no alcohol but there are a few alcoholic versions around.

Scent sensation

Orange flower water, distilled from the delicate white blooms of the orange blossom, gives sweet pear and redcurrant juices a delicate fragrance and "barely there" flavour. Like rose water, it's often associated with Middle Eastern cooking and goes really well with warm spices such as cinnamon.

Makes 4–5 glasses

4 pears

300g/11oz/2¾ cups redcurrants

2 cinnamon sticks

45ml/3 tbsp orange flower water

about 25g/1oz/¼ cup icing (confectioners') sugar

tonic water

cinnamon sticks (optional) and extra redcurrants, to decorate

Cut the pears into chunks and push through a juicer with the redcurrants. Crumble the cinnamon sticks into the juice, cover and leave to stand for at least 1 hour.

Strain the juice through a sieve into a bowl, then whisk in the orange flower water and a little icing sugar to taste.

To serve, put one or two cinnamon sticks in each glass, if using. Fill the glasses two-thirds full with the juice, then top up with tonic water and decorate with extra redcurrants.

To infuse with booze — This drink provides a fabulous change of flavour for those looking for an alcohol-free tipple but, if you want to add a splash of alcohol, try an almond liqueur such as Disaronno. The almondy edge goes very well with the scented fruit and flower flavours.

Grand marnier, papaya & passion fruit punch

The term "punch" comes from the Hindu word *panch* (five), relating to the five ingredients contained in the drink – alcohol, lemon or lime, tea, sugar and water. The ingredients may have altered somewhat over the years but the best punches still combine a mixture of spirits, flavourings and an innocent top-up of fizz or juice.

Makes about 15 glasses

2 large papayas

4 passion fruit

300g/11oz lychees, peeled and stoned (pitted)

300ml/½ pint/1¼ cups freshly squeezed orange juice

200ml/7fl oz/scant 1 cup grand marnier or other orange-flavoured liqueur

8 whole star anise

2 small oranges

ice cubes

1.5 litres/2½ pints/ 6 cups soda water (club soda)

Halve the papayas and discard the seeds. Halve the passion fruit and press the pulp through a sieve into a small punch bowl or a pretty serving bowl.

Push the papayas through a juicer, adding 100ml/3½fl oz/scant ½ cup water to help the pulp through. Juice the lychees. Add the juices to the bowl with the orange juice, liqueur and star anise. Thinly slice the oranges and add to the bowl. Chill for at least 1 hour or until ready to serve.

Add plenty of ice cubes to the bowl and top up with soda water. Ladle into punch cups or small glasses to serve.

Cucumber Pimm's punch

This tangy blend of freshly juiced cucumber, ginger and apples isn't as innocent as it looks – or tastes! It's lavishly topped with alcohol, so is definitely a drink to enjoy on a lazy summer's afternoon. To enjoy on a picnic, just chill the juice really well, then pour into a thermos flask and top up with chilled ginger ale when you reach your destination.

Makes 12 small glasses

1 cucumber

1 lemon

50g/2oz fresh root ginger

4 eating apples

600ml/1 pint/2½ cups Pimm's

sprigs of mint and borage

borage flowers

ice cubes

1.5 litres/2½ pints/6 cups ginger ale

Cut off a 5cm/2in length from the cucumber and thinly slice. Slice the lemon and set both aside.

Peel the remaining cucumber and cut it into large chunks. Roughly chop the ginger and apples. Push the apples, then the ginger and cucumber through a juicer and pour the juice into a large jug (pitcher) or bowl.

Stir the Pimm's into the juice and add the cucumber and lemon slices and the mint sprigs, then chill until ready to serve.

Just before serving, add the ice cubes and borage flowers to the punch and top up with ginger ale. Ladle into glasses or glass cups.

Borage flowers — These are the classic garnish for Pimm's but their season is fairly short so it's well worth freezing the tiny purple flowers in ice cubes for later in the summer when they're no longer available.

Light and yet temptingly moreish, this English classic is the ultimate thirst-quencher if you're out in the midday sun.

Cherry berry mull

Inspired by the traditional warm spices used to flavour mulled wine, this sweet and fruity punch makes a novel drink for barbecues and summer parties. Nothing brings out the irresistible flavours of soft summer fruits quite like juicing, and the orange liqueur and spices add a wonderfully rounded taste and feisty kick to the drink.

Makes 8 small glasses

2 cinnamon sticks, halved

15ml/1 tbsp whole cloves

15g/½oz/1 tbsp golden caster (superfine) sugar

300g/11oz/2¾ cups strawberries

150g/5oz/scant 1 cup raspberries

200g/7oz/scant 1 cup pitted cherries

150g/5oz/1¼ cups redcurrants

60ml/4 tbsp cointreau or other orange-flavoured liqueur

thinly sliced strawberries and raspberries, to decorate

extra cinnamon sticks for stirrers (optional)

Put the cinnamon sticks in a small pan with the cloves, sugar and 150ml/¼ pint/⅔ cup water. Heat gently until the sugar dissolves, then bring to the boil. Remove from the heat and leave to cool.

Push the strawberries, raspberries, cherries and redcurrants through a juicer and pour the juice into a large jug (pitcher).

Strain the cooled syrup through a sieve into the fruit juice, then stir in the liqueur. Add plenty of sliced fruits. Chill until needed. Serve in small glasses, with cinnamon stirrers, if you like.

Cherry berry bunches— For an outrageous decoration, tie a couple of cherry stalks to a stem of redcurrants and balance on the edge of each glass.

Warm spices and cool soft fruits go surprisingly well together. This unusual drink is perfect for *al fresco* drinking and is equally good without the alcohol.

Watermelon gin

The fabulously red, juicy flesh of the watermelon makes a perfect partner for the strong, heady scent and flavour of gin. The juice is so sweet and delicate, and this sparkling drink so stunningly pretty that you'll be hard-pressed to resist its appeal. For a party, just make up a large jug of the juice, top up with tonic and pour out for guests as they arrive.

Makes 4 large glasses

500g/1¼lb wedge watermelon

juice of 1 lime

10ml/2 tsp caster (superfine) sugar

crushed ice

150–200ml/5–7fl oz/
⅔–scant 1 cup gin

lime slices

tonic water

Cut off the skin from the watermelon and chop the flesh into large chunks, removing the seeds. Push the flesh through the juicer and pour into a large jug (pitcher). Stir in the lime juice and sugar and chill.

To serve, half-fill glasses with crushed ice. Stir the gin into the juice and pour over the ice. Add the lime slices and top up with tonic water.

Adding gin — Stir in gin to taste, as some people prefer it much stronger than others.

Lemon vodka

Very similar to the deliciously moreish Italian liqueur, Limoncello, this lemon vodka should be drunk in small quantities due to its hefty alcoholic punch. Blend the sugar, lemons and vodka and keep in a bottle in the refrigerator, ready for pouring over crushed ice, or topping up with soda or sparkling water. It is also delicious drizzled over melting vanilla ice cream.

Makes 12–15 glasses

10 large lemons

275g/10oz/generous 1¼ cups caster (superfine) sugar

250ml/8fl oz/1 cup vodka

Squeeze the lemons using a citrus juicer. Pour the juice into a jug (pitcher), add the sugar and whisk well until all the sugar has dissolved.

Strain the sweetened lemon juice into a thoroughly clean bottle or narrow-necked jar and add the vodka. Shake the mixture well to combine and chill for up to 2 weeks.

To serve, fill small glasses with ice and pour the lemon vodka over.

Making it minty— If you like, bruise a couple of mint leaves and add to the glass before pouring over the vodka.

Pure, clear vodka and sharp, zesty lemon juice make a tantalizing spirit that tastes like bottled sunshine.

Index

This edition is published by Aquamarine, an imprint of Anness Publishing Ltd, Hermes House, 88–89 Blackfriars Road, London SE1 8HA; tel. 020 7401 2077; fax 020 7633 9499

www.aquamarinebooks.com; www.annesspublishing.com

If you like the images in this book and would like to investigate using them for publishing, promotions or advertising, please visit our website www.practicalpictures.com for more information.

UK agent: The Manning Partnership Ltd; tel. 01225 478444; fax 01225 478440; sales@manning-partnership.co.uk
UK distributor: Grantham Book Services Ltd; tel. 01476 541080; fax 01476 541061; orders@gbs.tbs-ltd.co.uk
North American agent/distributor: National Book Network; tel. 301 459 3366; fax 301 429 5746; www.nbnbooks.com
Australian agent/distributor: Pan Macmillan Australia; tel. 1300 135 113; fax 1300 135 103; customer.service@macmillan.com.au
New Zealand agent/distributor: David Bateman Ltd; tel. (09) 415 7664; fax (09) 415 8892

Publisher: Joanna Lorenz
Managing Editor: Linda Fraser
Senior Editor: Susannah Blake
Copy Editor: Jenni Fleetwood
Editorial Reader: Richard McGinlay
Designer: Duncan Hemphill
Photographer: Gus Filgate
Home Economist: Silvana Franco
Stylist: Helen Trent
Production Controller: Ann Childers

ETHICAL TRADING POLICY
Because of our ongoing ecological investment programme, you, as our customer, can have the pleasure and reassurance of knowing that a tree is being cultivated on your behalf to naturally replace the materials used to make the book you are holding. For further information about this scheme, go to www.annesspublishing.com/trees

Notes
Bracketed terms are intended for American readers.

For all recipes, quantities are given in both metric and imperial measures and, where appropriate, measures are also given in standard cups and spoons. Follow one set, but not a mixture, because they are not interchangeable.

Standard spoon & cup measures are level.
1 tsp = 5ml, 1 tbsp = 15ml, 1 cup = 250ml/8fl oz
Australian standard tablespoons are 20ml. Australian readers should use 3 tsp in place of 1 tbsp for measuring small quantities of gelatine, flour, salt, etc.

Medium (US large) eggs are used unless otherwise stated.

Publisher's Acknowledgements
We would like to thank the following for the generous loan of equipment for photography: Magimix UK Limited and New Classics Limited for the loan of Waring products.